DISCERNING
GOD'S WILL

DISCERNING
GOD'S WILL

Richard T. Case

elevate
faith

Scripture taken from the NEW AMERICAN STANDARD BIBLE®, Copyright © 1960, 1962, 1963, 1968, 1971, 1972, 1973, 1975, 1977,1995 by The Lockman Foundation. Used by permission.

Published in Boise, Idaho by Elevate Faith, a division of Elevate Publishing. www.elevatepub.com.

For information please email: info@elevatepub.com.

ISBN (print): 9781943425457
Printed in the United States of America

Praise for *Discerning God's Will*

"I'm a big fan of Rich Case. Not only is he a fabulous human being, he is also the best Bible teacher I have ever met. When you read *Discerning God's Will*, you will learn how to move your life from ordinary to extraordinary by discovering what God's will really is for your life—and you will realize He is by your side to help make it happen. Thanks again, Rich, for opening my eyes to new possibilities through the power and love of our Father."

Ken Blanchard
Coauthor of *The New One Minute Manager®* and *Lead Like Jesus*

"Why do we think that God does not speak to us as He did the prophets of old? Why would He change? I am convinced that God's voice is just fine–it is our hearing that is impaired. In *Discerning God's Will*, Richard Case once again gives us practical methods to put our spirit in touch with God and shows us how to seek, listen and, in fact, hear from the Father. Well done!"

Michael Ducker
President and CEO, FedEx Freight
Vice Chair, U.S. Chamber of Commerce Board of Directors

"My sheep hear My voice…' The problem is that we sheep aren't very good listeners! In *Discerning God's Will*, Richard Case challenges us and equips us to know and better follow God. I'm grateful for this thoughtful, timely book from my long-time friend whose counsel, insights and example I've come to so greatly admire."

John D. Beckett
Chairman, The Beckett Companies
Author of *Loving Monday* and *Mastering Monday*

"If you want to know, love and serve God in this world and be happy with Him in the next, read this book. It will strengthen your spirit and give you a fresh guide to the wonder of God's love for you."

Jim Mudd
Founder, Mudd Advertising

"One of the most common and perplexing questions Christians ask is, 'How do I know if I am in the will of God?' Richard Case's book, *Discerning God's Will*, clearly and thoroughly takes us on a journey not only to learn how to hear and understand God's will, but to reveal the 'mystery' that He actually is working to manifest through His children! The truths in this book will release a new joy and enthusiasm in you as you hear directly from the Spirit and Word of God, the plans (His will) that He has for us."

Robert G. Rockwell
Founder & Managing Partner, AdviSoar LLC

"Richard T. Case is a trustworthy shepherd who, with great transparency, shares his vibrant joy and wisdom in what it means to live a life seeking and obeying God's will. *Discerning God's Will* is a thoughtful, scripturally based guide to the development of a practical interactive approach to seeking and obeying the will of God in the large and small aspects of life."

Phil Hodges
Cofounder, Lead Like Jesus

CONTENTS

INTRODUCTION:

Why is discerning God's will so problematic?

As Linda and I lead retreats, every participant, whether man or woman, always asks one set of questions: Does God actually have a will that involves me and is personal? If so, how do I discern God's will? Does it really matter? Isn't it too difficult to determine, and thus really just guess work?

People are all over the map on this. Most just see God as a creator with sovereignty that controls all things in life. It is a distant and overarching control that fulfills His eternal purposes. He has given us Scriptures, His principles and guidelines for living, which help define our requirements to attain eternal life. All of mankind has fallen short because of our sinful nature. Our only hope is to receive Jesus, His son, who died on the cross and was resurrected, as our Lord and Savior. Those who believe and receive Him get to go to heaven when they die. Those who don't believe and do not receive Jesus are eternally separated from God in hell. Those who are believers think that God puts the burden on us to live out His principles and guidelines as written in Scripture so that we might find a better life here in this world. However, there really is a belief that our life will be quite difficult. Because of our sinful nature, even though we try to be as good a Christian as we can, we often fail. This causes us to go to resignation and eventually settle for just doing our best within the confines of Biblical philosophy and guidelines. There are even many who involve themselves in an active Bible study and prayer but see little real fruit. Once in a while when things go well, we still expect the "other shoe to drop" and another

1

difficult situation to appear on the horizon. There certainly is little thought about God having a specific will that we can understand, and thus few even pursue knowing it.

There are others who do believe that God has a specific will for their life. Underneath it all, they struggle with understanding His will for the following reasons:

1. ***Think unknowable***–Though God has a will for us, we think that it is not really knowable since He does not speak to us in an audible voice. We already have a hard time understanding humans with which we can communicate directly. It is easy to feel that trying to discern God's will is beyond us.

2. ***Not clear, can't hear His voice well***–Sometimes we seem to be able to hear His voice and have some clarity. But most of the time His message seems neither precise nor clear, and hearing His voice is not something we experience daily. It seems confusing because our own voice and thoughts get in the way. Even in those rare times when our receptors for hearing God's will are working well, the enemy says things that further throws our listening into disarray. This can be exacerbated by all the different opinions that we receive from fellow Christians who, even with a good intent, try to give us advice. Sometimes, the more advice we receive, the more confused we become.

3. ***Not specific–isn't it up to us to just do our best?*** Many people who do believe that God has a will for us personally think that His will is rather broad in nature. It is more about principles and guidelines than anything specific. It seems untenable that God could or would speak specifics to us. That would require being able to directly hear His voice–which seems rather far-fetched. He has given us His will in the Scriptures through principles and guidelines. We should be able to evaluate or make a decision strict-

2

ly by that and do our best. If we have good hearts and attempt to base our decisions on the Bible, isn't that all God asks us to do? He understands our weaknesses and our inability to figure it all out, which is why He has such grace. We do understand that this life will be difficult, but hey, we get to go to heaven when we die.

4. *Just a matter of open and closed doors?* Most people do not believe that we can hear His voice personally. They feel God determines His specific will for us by simply opening and closing doors. We trust God, and thus if we just follow the path He creates through open and closed doors, will we not then be living out His will since He is sovereign and can open and close these doors? When there have been times that we seemingly went through open doors and it didn't work out too well, isn't that just God purposely causing us difficulty so that we can learn things and become transformed? Since He does have a plan, and He can open and close doors, it seems like the easiest way to go and never question the outcomes. That path creates two issues: First, when considering the intensity of our difficulties, we might find it hard to believe that God is always good. Second, it is easy to see that some people are blessed and others are not, which leads us to wonder why we are among those not blessed.

5. *Too complex, requires special wisdom*–Since determining God's will is so complex and mostly unknowable by the average Christian, many think that there are super-spiritual people that have special insight into God's will for us. So, our thought is that if we truly desire to know God's will, our best plan of action is to seek out the best possible super-spiritual person that hopefully can give us advice that will be in line with God's will. We do not think that we would ever hear God speaking directly to

us, so we go to a more skilled intermediary who has better spiritual gifts. The main problem with this particular approach is that it's difficult to locate such super-spiritual people, and when we find someone they often disappoint us. Their wisdom doesn't necessarily translate into better things for us.

6. *Hasn't panned out before*–In many cases, we thought we did have an understanding of God's will and it just didn't pan out. After we prayed, spent time in the Word and asked others' advice, we felt confident that we had a sense of clarity about God's will and what to do. We did it thinking it was God's will, and it still just didn't turn out well. Since this has occurred more than once, it goes back to either thinking that God's will is really unknowable, or God really isn't very good and we happen to be one of the unlucky ones. Therefore, why bother attempting to pursue God's will–isn't it better to just do our best and figure things out on our own anyway?

7. *Not sure how character fits in or how important it is*– For those to claim to know God's will, it seems to me that they have many lapses of good character and often seem rather hypocritical. What they claim to be God's will looks more like self-determination. It benefits them with little regard for others, particularly when it seems to negatively impact others or hurt others. So we wonder if character matters in this regard and how important it is, if at all. Further, if character really does matter, then how does God's will relate to Christians who have character issues and even severe problems? Do we have to reach a certain level of Christian maturity before we are able to understand God's will, and does our lack of maturity prevent us from understanding God's will?

8. *Too anxious, can't wait*–We live in a fast-paced world where decisions need to be made quickly. We just don't have the time to gain any sense of clarity about God's will, and we just are too anxious to get moving to spend any time on trying. We know that if we delay, others will make many decisions for us. It is just easier not to attempt to include this in our decision-making process. So we try to gather as many facts as possible to do our own evaluation and make the best judgment we can. We know that we often will not make the right decisions, but if we try hard enough we might still have a pretty good batting average. Isn't that a good thing?

This book is intended to demonstrate, from God's very Scriptures, the truth about God's will–that it is:

1. Personal and planned out specifically for us.

2. Fully knowable–we can hear His voice and receive His will.

3. Clear and precise–very specific.

4. Simple and beautiful.

5. Involves the transformation of our "character"–so all can know His voice from the most immature to the very mature Christian.

6. The best and none better–He is for us, has fantastic plans for us and invites us to experience a blessed life.

7. Not limited to opening and closing doors.

8. Perfect in its timing–and timing is everything.

If everyone can truly receive these truths, they will find that their life lifts from a struggle in mediocrity to a spectacular, exceptional life. In this book, you will find the biggest "Ah ha" moment is when you understand that God's will is not so much about what *we* are to do, but rather what He wants to do to lead us to the spectacular life. He invites us to join Him as He leads and guides us to specific places where the spectacular life plays out. May you enjoy receiving a whole new way of walking with God in your life.

EXERCISE:

Before you work through the book, write out in a separate journal the current decisions and issues you are facing, along with any questions for which you are seeking to discern God's will. Through each step, use these real situations in your life to help you move from theoretical and interesting to real and valuable. Keep "journaling" your prayers, your insights, your thoughts and conclusions after processing each chapter. This will greatly assist you in fully understanding how receiving God's will is so practical and personal.

1
WHAT EXACTLY IS GOD'S WILL?

Luke 11:1-13:

1 Now it came to pass, as He was praying in a certain place, when He ceased, that one of His disciples said to Him, "Lord, teach us to pray, as John also taught his disciples." 2 So He said to them, "When you pray, say: Our Father in heaven, Hallowed be Your name. Your kingdom come. Your will be done On earth as it is in heaven. 3 Give us day by day our daily bread. 4 And forgive us our sins, For we also forgive everyone who is indebted to us. And do not lead us into temptation, But deliver us from the evil one." 5 And He said to them, "Which of you shall have a friend, and go to him at midnight and say to him, 'Friend, lend me three loaves; 6 for a friend of mine has come to me on his journey, and I have nothing to set before him'; 7 and he will answer from within and say, 'Do not trouble me; the door is now shut, and my children are with me in bed; I cannot rise and give to you'? 8 I say to you, though he will not rise and give to him because he is his friend, yet because of his persistence he will rise and give him as many as he needs. 9 "So I say to you, ask, and it will be given to you; seek, and you will find; knock, and it will be opened to you. 10 For everyone who asks receives, and he who seeks finds, and to him who knocks it will be opened. 11 If a son asks for bread from any father among you, will he give him a stone? Or if he asks for a fish, will he give him a serpent instead of a fish? 12 Or if he asks for an egg, will he offer him a scorpion? 13 If you then, being evil, know how to give good gifts to your children, how much more will your heavenly Father give the Holy Spirit to those who ask Him!"

Jesus' disciples asked Him how to pray. After honoring the Father and recognizing the magnificence of the Father, He first states to ask for two things:

1. Thy kingdom come

2. Thy will be done

Think of the significance of this: If the kingdom was here and His will was always operating, there would be no reason for us to ask for it—it would be meaningless. Rather, Christ specifically says that we are to ask for His kingdom and His will to be done in our personal circumstances. This also implies two more important things in this request, namely that:

1. God has a kingdom.

2. God has a will.

THY KINGDOM COME:

God's kingdom is an interesting dynamic to understand. The kingdom that all people are born into with their sinful nature, comprised of flesh and a soul (what in the Scriptures is stated as "heart"—the seat of the will, mind, intellect, emotions, and personality—devoid of the Holy Spirit), is Satan's kingdom. When Jesus was tempted as described in Luke 4:5-8, Satan offered Christ the kingdoms of the world which had been delivered to him; they were delivered to him by Adam and Eve who disobeyed God's instructions and ate of the tree of the knowledge of good and evil. When they did, they died as God had spoken. What died was their inherent spiritual connection to God. All subsequent offspring inherited this sinful nature, flesh and soul, dominated by self—separated from God. They also were removed from the Garden of Eden, which was God's kingdom. Through this "fall" into a life of sin, they delivered to Satan the operation of the world; as John 10:10 says, "The thief comes to kill, steal and destroy—everything is going to destruction and everything in life will be a struggle."

The only remedy for restoring God's kingdom is to be born again—where we once again receive His Holy Spirit. From the time we are born again we have a daily choice to make; namely to walk in the Spirit or by default walk back in the self (called being carnal). When we operate carnally as described in Romans 8:5-8, we again put to death the

8

spiritual connectivity; we are at enmity against God and cannot please Him. In essence, we have moved back into Satan's kingdom and are not operating in God's kingdom. Since there is a kingdom, it implies a king–God–who rules supreme and fulfills His purposes. Our entrance to and living in the kingdom of God is based upon our surrender of our will to His will. He is to fully be King, and we are to fully be servants–His special servants because we are children of and friends with the King. We have special privileges and rights. So, as Jesus revealed in His instructions on prayer, we are to ask for His kingdom to come.

He is saying that we are to surrender our will to His, to enjoy the benefits of His kingdom, and to live out the planned life that the King has for us. (An important footnote: we are not exempt from Satan's kingdom and the consequences of Satan's kingdom.) We will experience trouble, as Christ described in John 16:33, but if we live in God's kingdom as we march through Satan's worldly kingdom, we will experience the magnificence of God's rule and the power to overcome anything that the enemy can throw at us. It is only when we step outside of God's rule that we cannot reconcile how things can become so difficult with a supposedly good God. It just doesn't make sense to us. Therefore, what happens is that we go to a place of resignation and actually develop hardness toward God. (This is my lot in life, I might as well put up with it because then I get to go to heaven.) The consequence of walking in the enemy's kingdom is life with no hope of restoration. This is why God has told us to ask for His kingdom to come. It should be and is a high priority in our daily prayer life–and understanding that it is a surrender of our will to His, we stay in that place of surrender.

THY WILL BE DONE:

Since "Thy kingdom come" is contingent upon our surrender of our will to His will, the second element that Christ tells us to pray for is, "Thy will be done." This implies specifically that He has a will, and we are to ask for His will to be fulfilled in us and in the circumstances of our life. By definition, we need to hear, receive, understand and be

9

obedient to His will. Further, He makes a declarative statement about His will being done: It is to be done on earth as it is in heaven. This is a most profound statement. How is His will done in heaven? Perfectly! The heavenly host and the angels have specific assignments–to move between heaven and earth (one dimension to the other) and minister to us. They are to provide instruction, intervention, guidance, supernatural work, etc. Since they are personal to us, God's will is personal to us. He gives them specific instructions for how they are to carry out their assignments in our life so that we can join Him in what He wants to do. Since they are completely surrendered (their will to His will), God's will in heaven is fulfilled completely and perfectly. We on earth are to live in the same manner–to have His will be done completely and perfectly. Remember that this is not automatic or we would not have to ask for it. This means that as we live in His kingdom through surrender of our will to His will, we are then to walk in such a way that we fully hear, receive, understand and carry out this will.

If it were not specific to us, we would never know if this prayer is answered. Most believers live with this thought: that everything is God's will and what will be–will be. This is called Christian fatalism. It takes us out of the equation and basically puts us in a position where we are living this struggle of mediocrity and resigned to a difficult life. Living in fatalism greatly hinders our understanding of what God desires for us–a loving grand plan designed especially for us. We can actually move out of God's kingdom through self and into Satan's kingdom where these difficulties are actually occurring. Fatalism carries us to a false understanding of life–that we are always in His kingdom and under His control, and thus all that happens is ordained by God.

Again, think of the simplicity of this Prayer: We have to ask for God's kingdom and for His will to be done. We have to understand that not everything that happens to us is God's will. Rather, He is so sovereign that upon us asking for His kingdom through surrender of our will and then learning to follow His will, He can redeem and restore anything at anytime. This is the good news.

Further, we are to recognize that this will is very personal:

Luke 11:2 specifically says that we are to pray to "Our Father," who is omnipotent, omnipresent, omniscient, loving and caring. God is called the Father of the stars, the heavenly luminaries, because He is their creator, upholder and ruler. He is also the Father of all rational and intelligent beings, whether angels or men, because He is their creator, preserver, guardian and protector. Christians, through Christ, have been exalted to an especially close and intimate relationship with God. We no longer dread Him as a stern judge of sinners, but revere Him as our reconciled and loving Father, the Father of Jesus Christ. We are to "hallow" Him as sacred and holy–to be honored and followed. Though He is creator and sovereign, we are not to address Him solely as God the creator, but rather as Father. "Father" implies that we are His children and have a special privilege and relationship with our Father. As parents, we deeply care for our children and have a will to bring them to a good and grand life. Our Father is infinitely bigger and has more care than us. It is personal, He loves us, He has grand plans for us and wants us to enjoy the fullness of life here on earth with Him.

Psalm 139:1-10; 15-18; 23-24: He knows me intimately and has already written (ordained) my days.

1 For the Chief Musician. A Psalm of David. O Lord, You have searched me and known me. 2 You know my sitting down and my rising up; You understand my thoughts afar off. 3 You comprehend my path and my lying down, And are acquainted with all my ways. 4 For there is not a word on my tongue, But behold, O Lord, You know it altogether. 5 You have hedged me behind and before, And laid Your hand upon me. 6 Such knowledge is too wonderful for me; It is high, I cannot attain it. 7 Where can I go from Your Spirit? Or where can I flee from Your presence? 8 If I ascend into heaven, You are there; If I make my bed in hell, behold, You are there. 9 If I take the wings of the morning, And dwell in the uttermost parts of the sea, 10 Even there Your hand shall lead me, And Your right hand shall hold me.... 15 My frame was not hidden from You, When I was made in secret, And skillfully wrought in the lowest parts of the earth. 16 Your eyes saw my substance, being yet unformed. And in Your book they all were written, The days fashioned for me, When as yet there were none of them. 17 How precious also are Your thoughts to me, O God! How great is the sum of them! 18 If I should count them, they would be more in number than the sand; When I awake, I am still with You…. 23 Search me, O God, and know my heart; Try me, and know my anxieties; 24 And see if there is any wicked way in me, And lead me in the way everlasting.

His will is not merely some overriding set of principles and guidelines, but rather is geared specifically for each one of us. He knows us intimately and has already ordained each day of our lives (His will). He has planned a specific path for each of us to walk, and He desires to guide us along that path. Because of His love, He also allows us to choose to not walk the ordained day He has planned. (Again, this is why we have to ask for it and live in it.) Nevertheless, these days are already planned, and His sovereignty is so great that He ordains each next day from where we are today. If we've lived our life away from His kingdom and on our own and never experienced His ordained specific path for us, He asks us a wonderful question: How about now? God can sovereignly restore, redeem and bring us to the fullness of His ordained plan, again, which is specific to us. Further, He invites us to a much larger story to join Him in His purposes and work of expanding His kingdom and being part of His covenant life. We become blessed to become a blessing (we will explore this more later).

Psalm 23; John 10:3-5; 27: My Shepherd cares for me, leads me, knows me by name, I am special to Him.

Psalm 23:1 A Psalm of David. The Lord is my shepherd; I shall not want. 2 He makes me to lie down in green pastures; He leads me beside the still waters. 3 He restores my soul; He leads me in the paths of righteousness For His name's sake. 4 Yea, though I walk through the valley of the shadow of death, I will fear no evil; For You are with me; Your rod and Your staff, they comfort me 5 You prepare a table before me in the presence of my enemies; You anoint my head with oil; My cup runs over. 6 Surely goodness and mercy shall follow me All the days of my life; And I will dwell in the house of the Lord Forever.

John 10:3 To him the doorkeeper opens, and the sheep hear his voice; and he calls his own sheep by name and leads them out. 4 And when he brings out his own sheep, he goes before them; and the sheep follow him, for they know his voice. 5 Yet they will by no means follow a stranger, but will flee from him, for they do not know the voice of strangers."...27 My sheep hear My voice, and I know them, and they follow Me.

We are to recognize that He is not just any shepherd or even only just "the" Shepherd. He is "My Shepherd;" personal because we are His personal sheep. This means that we have a unique relationship to the Shepherd. We are special to Him and receive special attention. We are intimate so that our relationship is filled with love, admiration, emotion, excitement and truth. The Shepherd desires to be in fellowship with us–communicating His affection for us and inviting us to communicate that back. As a result of this special relationship, we have beautiful benefits promised by "My Shepherd":

♦ *MY Shepherd–We have a special and intimate relationship*

♦ *I shall not want. (Why? He promises abundant life–John 10:10.)*

♦ *Makes me lie down in green pastures–His will includes and is centered upon rest and refreshment–where we enjoy life the best.*

♦ *Leads me beside still waters–He knows we need nourishment, sustenance; and is the provider of everything we need.*

♦ *Restores my soul–My Shepherd knows that my sinful nature and my past has damaged my soul. I carry lies, wounds, heaviness and burdens because of the damage to my soul. My Shepherd works around and through me to bring healing health and full restoration so that my life is full of freedom and joy.*

13

- *Though I walk in a difficult world (the enemy is always working against me, and since we are walking in enemy territory—we will have trouble and adversity):*

  - *I will not fear. (He will take care of me; the enemy is not able to succeed against me.)*

  - *Experience that He is with me—I am safe and protected.*

  - *His rod and staff (weapons against the enemy) will protect me and I can be comforted completely.*

- *I get to feast with joy and peace in the middle of this difficult world—all prepared by Him. Difficult circumstances are not to dominate our lives, but we are to enjoy the fullness of His will as normal.*

- *I will be anointed—set apart to experience the Holy Spirit fully in my life—and will be overflowing (with all of the Spirit in me).*

- *Goodness (His good for my life) and mercy (freedom and joy as I walk with Him, not burdened by my mistakes and failures) will fill my life—all the days of my life.*

- *I get to dwell (abide) with Him always.*

As His sheep, we have an amazing PERSONAL privilege. **He speaks to us personally, not through stilted theology or vague concepts, but we actually hear HIM—what He specifically has to speak to us personally.**

- **If we are hearing His voice, what is He doing?** *Speaking, talking to us, discussing with us and communicating personally.*

- **What are the characteristics of hearing His voice?** *Personal—He calls us by name (knows us and all about us), leads us. We clearly know it is Him and not something else; gives us clarity to follow HIM.*

- **How will we recognize the difference between His voice and others (Satan's, ours, other people's well meaning advice)?** *We will know the difference because there is a unique sound, a unique quality, a resonating truth and the application of that truth through the Spirit within us. It will not be fuzzy or confusing. It will be very clear and distinctive, always lining up with the truth in the Word and creating in us a feeling of righteousness, peace and joy.*

- **What is necessary to recognize His voice?** *We must spend time in His presence, experiencing His voice—think of a baby who quickly learns to recognize the voice of his/her mother and father. How does this work? By just hearing it over and over again. Same for us with Christ. Just be with HIM, hearing His voice over and over again until we fully recognize the difference between His voice and the enemy's, our own, or other peoples' good advice.*

We must understand that it is important to know our personal Father, our Shepherd by being with Him, hearing His voice, and asking for His kingdom to come; His will to be done—on earth (in our personal life) as it is in heaven.

The key to it all is this: His will is a person, not a principle. It is Him in Him, in His kingdom, through Him. What an amazing privilege we have.

In 1992, Linda and I were living in Boulder, Colorado—a most beautiful place. I was enjoying work as a management consultant and our life in Boulder with skiing, hiking, biking and raising our children in the mountains. We also were leaders of a young marriage class at our local church. The Lord had grown the class from nothing to 50 couples who were learning to walk with God and hear His voice. We noticed that few of them went to church worship, so we inquired as to why they were attending the class but not going to church. The answer was that the music was not interesting to them because it was very traditional hymns with organ and choir. Our leader committee met, and we believed that we could assist the church transition one of their services (they had three) to a contemporary service.

In our class we had fantastic musicians and singers. We went to the church leadership and made the request. We volunteered to provide all of the music and worship leading–and fit it to the messages that the pastor normally gave in the other two services. At that time, the leadership of the church was stuck on traditional music and said that they would not consider such a transition, and that it might be a better idea if we started a new church. So our committee met and prayed, and we heard God direct us to work toward starting a new church.

Our leadership group met for six months, praying that God would send a pastor willing to start a new church to join us in this ministry. The following month, the group came to Linda and I and said that God had told them that we were to be the pastors to start it. (I was a seminary graduate, an ordained minister, and had helped start a church in the 70s.) Though Linda and I had not heard that instruction, we went to prayer and asked God to confirm to us the message that He spoke to the group. We did hear a "yes," but because I had a thriving business and wondered if it truly was possible, we prayed that if this was truly His will, He would bring at least 20 people that had already been part of a church plant to assist us. (None of the young marrieds had ever been engaged in such an endeavor.) Within a month, we had sitting in our living room 28 people, who had all been part of church plants and had moved from California, Texas and Illinois to Colorado.

These newcomers shared God's vision and were excited about being part of another church plant. At that meeting, we established a statement of beliefs and our uniqueness, and then asked the group when they would like to start. They responded with, "How about next week?" So, that's what we did. Within two months, we grew out of the house location into the local YMCA. Within two more months, we grew out of that and had to move to a school auditorium. (The Boulder school system openly rented space on weekends to churches at very favorable rates.) It was quite a start to God's work as we heard His voice, followed Him as our Shepherd, and together witnessed an amazing work of God as He brought gifted people to intimate relationship with Himself, and then gave them the heart to "give it away."

2

HIS WILL IS ALL ABOUT HIS PLANS FOR US–TO LIVE OUT HIS BIGGER STORY

Jeremiah 29:11-14: Plans–a Hope and a Future.

11 For I know the thoughts that I think toward you, says the Lord, thoughts of peace and not of evil, to give you a future and a hope. 12 Then you will call upon Me and go and pray to Me, and I will listen to you. 13 And you will seek Me and find Me, when you search for Me with all your heart. 14 I will be found by you, says the Lord, and I will bring you back from your captivity; I will gather you from all the nations and from all the places where I have driven you, says the Lord, and I will bring you to the place from which I caused you to be carried away captive.

God clearly states that He knows the plans He has for us. By definition, plans mean that they are prepared ahead of time. So God has prepared ahead of time a unique plan for each of us. This is not a generic or theological plan, but rather a very specific detailed plan of our daily activity and paths/decisions we are to take. He knows what His will is each and every day; each and every step. There is a beautiful quality about these plans–they are plans for peace (Shalom), hope and a future. Peace (Shalom) in the Hebrew specifically means: *welfare, health, prosperity, quiet, tranquility and contentment.* He wants us to fully understand that His plans are nothing but good–for our favor, for our benefit, and for His glory. He also states that they are not for evil, which does not actually mean demonic but rather: *bad, unpleasant, evil (giving pain, unhappiness, misery) displeasing, bad (of its kind–land, water, etc.), bad (of value), worse than, worst (comparison), sad, unhappy, evil (hurtful), distress, adversity.* His will for our life is intended to bring us into Shalom and to prevent us from moving into evil–things that are going to frustrate, annoy and be difficult. As we realize the nature of these plans, we will willingly and excitedly pursue these plans–plans for a hope (positive expectation, good outcome) and a future–what is ahead is good. Since He knows these plans, and needs for us to walk into these plans, it is rather simple to realize that we must receive, understand and be able to clearly follow His will.

Covenant: Genesis 12:1-3; Deuteronomy 28:1-15; Psalms 25:14: Blessed to be a blessing.

Genesis 12:1 Now the Lord had said to Abram: "Get out of your country, From your family And from your father's house, To a land that I will show you. 2 I will make you a great nation; I will bless you And make your name great; And you shall be a blessing. 3 I will bless those who bless you, And I will curse him who curses you; And in you all the families of the earth shall be blessed."

An important truth of God's plans is that they are rooted in His covenant promise to His sheep–all of us are to be blessed to become a blessing. Blessing in the Hebrew means: *prosperity, to do or give something of value to another.* Galatians 3:15-18 tells us that we are still recipients of this covenant–Christ is the fulfillment of this covenant and has fully received this promise. We then have the privilege of fully experiencing this promise as we walk in Christ. His plans are intended to place us where we can be blessed and then join Him in His bigger story as we "give it away" and become a blessing to others. This is fundamental to all believers' lives. It should be noted that there is also a key provision to this covenant promise–that those who bless us will be blessed and those who curse us will be cursed. This is why Romans 12:9-20 speaks to our role when people oppose us or, in essence, curse us. Cursing us means: *to slight, be swift in dismissing us, be trifling with us, hold us of little account, hold us in contempt or dishonor us.* God says that we can count on Him cursing them, and thus we do not need to take any action or be hostile back, but rather to realize that "vengeance is His sayeth the Lord." Thus, our focus needs to be walking in His will where we can receive His blessings, be a blessing to others and not fret about those who get in the way. His plans include taking care of them so that they do not continue to affect us and diminish His abundant blessings.

19

Deuteronomy 28:1-14:

Deuteronomy 28:1 Now it shall come to pass, if you diligently obey the voice of the Lord your God, to observe carefully all His commandments which I command you today, that the Lord your God will set you high above all nations of the earth. 2 And all these blessings shall come upon you and overtake you, because you obey the voice of the Lord your God: 3 Blessed shall you be in the city, and blessed shall you be in the country. 4 Blessed shall be the fruit of your body, the produce of your ground and the increase of your herds, the increase of your cattle and the offspring of your flocks. 5 Blessed shall be your basket and your kneading bowl. 6 Blessed shall you be when you come in, and blessed shall you be when you go out. 7 "The Lord will cause your enemies who rise against you to be defeated before your face; they shall come out against you one way and flee before you seven ways. 8 The Lord will command the blessing on you in your storehouses and in all to which you set your hand, and He will bless you in the land which the Lord your God is giving you. 9 The Lord will establish you as a holy people to Himself, just as He has sworn to you, if you keep the commandments of the Lord your God and walk in His ways. 10 Then all peoples of the earth shall see that you are called by the name of the Lord, and they shall be afraid of you. 11 And the Lord will grant you plenty of goods, in the fruit of your body, in the increase of your livestock, and in the produce of your ground, in the land of which the Lord swore to your fathers to give you. 12 The Lord will open to you His good treasure, the heavens, to give the rain to your land in its season, and to bless all the work of your hand. You shall lend to many nations, but you shall not borrow. 13 And the Lord will make you the head and not the tail; you shall be above only, and not be beneath, if you heed the commandments of the Lord your God, which I command you today, and are careful to observe them. 14 So you shall not turn aside from any of the words which I command you this day, to the right or the left, to go after other gods to serve them. 15 "But it shall come to pass, if you do not obey the voice of the Lord your God, to observe carefully all His commandments and His statutes which I command you today, that all these curses will come upon you and overtake you:

"The Father" lays out a series of specific blessings as part of this Covenant Promise:

- In the city and in the country; and when we go in and out (wherever we are)

- Offspring (children and grandchildren)

- Our work—our occupation—whatever we put our hand to

- Our provision—blessings on our storehouses (we will have plenty)

- Enemies to be defeated

- Intimacy with God

- Identified as followers of God and carry His power

- Be lenders and not borrowers

- Head and not the tail (be led by the Spirit and not the world)

- Above and not beneath (experiencing the power of God and not subject to the world)

- Serve only God

Psalms 25:14:
Psalm 25:14 The secret of the Lord is with those who fear Him, And He will show them His covenant.

He reiterates His promise that He will show us His covenant. Thus, we should expect to experience all of these specific terms of the covenant that are on His heart to show. This is not to be only an intellectual understanding of the blessings of the covenant, but rather we are to experience this in our real life.

John 10:10; Psalm 65:11: Abundant life.

John 10:10 The thief does not come except to steal, to kill, and to destroy. I have come that they may have life, and that they may have it more abundantly.

Psalm 65:11 You crown the year with Your goodness, And Your paths drip with abundance.

Christ states that His primary purpose is to give us abundant life–now. Actually, He says that it will be super abundant–over-the-top fantastically extraordinary. In Psalm 65:11, the Father promises us that He will crown us with goodness along with our paths–His plans for us; His will for us–will overflow with abundance. His desire (His will for us) is to give (deliver to) us this superabundant life and for us to experience this gift during our earthly lives. He wants us to have, own, possess and hold firmly the wonders of this life; to experience completely the full, genuine, real, active, vigorous, fullness of the life of God, and to enjoy it more abundantly; exceedingly, supremely, extraordinarily, more remarkably, more excellently. IT IS TRULY AMAZING–THIS LIFE THAT HE GIVES US IS TO BE EXCEPTIONAL IN ALL REGARDS. WHEN: NOW. What if I have blown my life, made mistakes or I'm not in a great place? NO MATTER, HOW ABOUT ALLOWING HIM TO GIVE YOU THIS ABUNDANT LIFE NOW? Further, He tells us that the goodness He has planned for us is pleasant, agreeable (to the senses), pleasing (to the higher nature), excellent (of its kind), rich, valuable in estimation, glad, happy, prosperous (of man's sensuous nature), good understanding (of man's intellectual nature), beneficial, for our welfare, prosperity, and happiness.

I hope that this is really sinking in. Many people believe that because of their difficult life with lots of unanswered prayers, any statements about God's will being spectacular just don't seem to ring true. We must understand that His will is by imitation. As we learned from Luke in the Lord's Prayer, we must ask for His will to be done; which means that we allow Him to be King, and we are to surrender to His instructions as we live in His kingdom. Most people do not experience a spectacular life because they are approaching their relationship with the King on an intellectual basis by trying to perform on their own power. They choose to not believe that God's will is noble, and thus are relegated to live in it the best they can–which is not great. In order for us to experience His will, we must get settled in our minds that His plans are good; that He desires to give us superabundant life and that He has goodness for us.

Church plant–continued:

As we continue the story of the church plant, our leaders and members were enjoying our collective walk into the beautiful abundant life given by our Father. Times were exciting! Lots of miracles, transformation, joy as a community and more and more people joining God's work. Every week for church, we had to cart our worship gear in from the trailer at 6:00 a.m. into the school auditorium and classrooms for the kids. The facilities were adequate but "dumpy." Someone mentioned that we ought to approach the University of Colorado and see if we could use one of its auditoriums, all of which were first-class. The University said that because of separation of church and state they could not rent their auditoriums to a church. I asked that if I rented it to speak on the environment each week if they would rent it to me. They said yes. I challenged them, asking if they thought this was being fair? They agreed it wasn't, but said rules were rules. To change the rules I had to appeal to the regents of the university. So, I wrote a well-thought-out letter explaining why I believed it would be fair to rent to a church. I personally didn't hold much hope and had little faith, but the team all believed that God said he would make the crooked places straight. I expected a letter from the university's attorneys, who would explain why it was not legally possible.

Rather, a month later I received a phone call that they had agreed that it was not fair and that I could choose any room that I wanted at the university. I said, "How about the planetarium?" They agreed. The University of Colorado rented the planetarium to us for $150 per week with $10.5 million worth of equipment, including the "star-maker" that produces all the constellations onto the circular ceiling and 105 projectors. They allowed us to keep all of our Sunday school partitions and supplies behind the equipment–truly miraculous. Because we could create anything that we could dream up (they allowed us to work with their programmers), we began our first worship at the planetarium on Easter Sunday. We advertised sunrise service at 10:00 a.m., and it was packed out. When the congregation walked in, it was night and the stars were out. After we began our first worship song and everyone was seated, the sun rose and we created a story of the resurrection, including showing Jesus on the cross and being resurrected. It was spectacular and a service that no one will ever forget. Because of the skill of our programmers, they could produce anything that we could imagine. For example, we wanted a winter scene in the woods with the church in the background with lighted stained-glass windows and the horse and buggy driving in the snow with caroling–done! We truly had spectacular visuals for our worship services. We all knew that the abundant life was not related to a church plant or us building a church; rather, it was following His will and specific assignment for us as He delivered this abundant life to us as a community.

3
HIS PLAN IS AN INVITATION FOR US TO JOIN HIM IN HIS BIGGER STORY

It is important to understand that though we tend to view God's will as strictly personal and what do we need to do, He is always moving us into His bigger purposes and story–which is redemption, restoration and having His born-again children experience the fullness of His good plans. As we have learned in the discussion on covenant, we are blessed to become a blessing. We will always be involved with receiving and giving blessings away. As subjects in His kingdom, we are called to serve the King and to fulfill the purposes of the King. The Father wishes to expand His kingdom, and thus will involve us in that activity. It is to be considered an honor and pure joy to be co-laborers in His greater story.

1 Samuel 2:35:
35 Then I will raise up for Myself a faithful priest who shall do according to what is in My heart and in My mind. I will build him a sure house, and he shall walk before My anointed forever.

He calls us to be faithful priests and to do what is IN God's heart and mind as we walk with HIM. To be faithful means to be reliable, trustworthy and obedient to His instruction and to live out His will. This means we first have to understand His will and then fully embrace His will. Interestingly, a priest's first duty is to minister to God. He is to praise and worship, hear His voice, and understand fully His assignments. As we understand God's heart and mind, we will be fulfilling these assignments as faithful priests.

And we know that His assignments are always intended to be part of a bigger story–impacting others and expanding His kingdom. Thus, it is not all about us, but rather about joining Him in His eternal purposes. Later, in chapter five, we will highlight that we are not to dream up our own thoughts of what would be helpful for the ministry of the kingdom—which is how most believers operate. They do have a heart for ministry, but they actually are operating outside of God's will as they are dreaming up their own thoughts and ideas for how to carry it out, and thus lack both the effectiveness and the power—because they are not walking in God's will.

Matthew 28:18-20:

18 And Jesus came and spoke to them, saying, "All authority has been given to Me in heaven and on earth. 19 Go therefore and make disciples of all the nations, baptizing them in the name of the Father and of the Son and of the Holy Spirit, 20 teaching them to observe all things that I have commanded you; and lo, I am with you always, even to the end of the age." Amen.

His good plan involves transferring His authority to us as we join Him in making disciples (followers of Him into His bigger story and His specific plan for them)—teaching (dialoguing) to follow His instructions (His will). God's authority involves superior power over earthly things. By definition, this involves the miraculous and the supernatural. The miraculous is not intended to just be experienced alone, but rather in the broader context of God's eternal purposes of making disciples. It is important to note that making disciples is a universal call for all believers and not limited to just teachers or pastors. As we are living as disciples experiencing his supernatural power, we are to invite others to join us and learn what we are learning—to receive and experience His will, which is both spectacular for us and intended to be part of a bigger story.

Ephesians 2:10:

10 For we are His workmanship, created in Christ Jesus for good works, which God prepared beforehand that we should walk in them.

We are His workmanship; created IN Christ Jesus for good (exceptional) works, prepared beforehand that we should walk in them (His will). As we more fully understand His will, we realize that He is working in us so that we might be transformed and experience His goodness and then fulfill His works, which He prepared beforehand. This is why it is so critical to live out His will; He has prepared in advance the path He wishes us to take. It is very specific and very personal to us. He has it all planned out. This, again, is why we need to understand that what He considers good is His plan and not ours. We may come up with what we believe to be "good" things to do for God, but His good plans are His plans, not ours. We are to truly be His workmanship–let Him do the work of fulfilling His will in and through us.

Church plant–continued:

As we were experiencing God's will and the abundant life granted to us, we had no idea of the much bigger story that we were being invited to join. When we were still in the school, another local church approached us to consider taking them over as they were failing financially. Their pastor had not received a salary in several months, and they were behind on their bills. We prayed as we sought God's will and heard a confirmation to proceed. Since all of us were volunteers, none of us took salaries, and thus we had very few expenses.

As a result, the generous giving of the congregation was put into savings and we had accumulated close to $100,000. This cash gave us the ability to pay the other church's past-due bills, past-due salaries, and even give a generous severance to the pastor. The church did have two assets, which came with the takeover–a building and 10 acres of land in downtown Louisville, a nearby community to Boulder. The building was not adequate for us to move into, so we put it on the market. It sold over a year later and we put the money in the bank. We gave little thought to the 10 acres and just held onto it.

As we grew in the planetarium, we reached a point where Linda and I knew I had to either step in as a full-time pastor or return to my consulting business and recruit a full-time pastor. Through prayer we heard, "Well done, faithful servant; thanks, but your assignment is over and you are to return to consulting and recruit a new pastor." A wonderful pastor and his family from Illinois joined us and stepped into the full-time senior pastor role. He was a gifted preacher and over the next several years grew the church to several thousand attendees. (By this time, Linda and I had left and wound up stepping into another pastoral role in a troubled church.)

As our original start-up church grew to an even larger size, they required more space. They located an empty building that once had been a department store and found that it was perfect for their next jump up in space. However, the county would not allow them to occupy the store as they needed the tax revenue from sales from another store that they expected to move in. The church leaders prayed and, again, God said that he would make the crooked places straight.

Someone on the Council discovered that the church owned 10 acres in Louisville (which we had received from the other church that had struggled but had done nothing with). The county made a proposal to the church that they would allow the church to occupy the department store for seven years and that they would trade the 10 acres for 25 acres out in the country. God confirmed with a big "yes," and they traded the property and moved into the department store. The church kept growing and, eventually, a new pastor replaced the second pastor who had replaced me.

Under his leadership, the church grew to over 10,000 people and were then in a position to put together a building program on the 25 acres. Today, this church (Flatirons Community Church) is over 20,000 people and occupies 165,000 ft.^{2} of buildings on that same 25 acres. In the beginning, we believed that we were being called into a bigger story but had no idea that the steps of God's will along the way would lead to such a magnificent story. We were all privileged to join this bigger story and to see it unfold. Last Easter, the church baptized over 1,800 people. How cool is that?

4

THIS PLAN IS ALREADY LAID OUT IN HIMSELF & HIS WORD (both New and Old Testament)–TRUTH

We all wish to understand and live out God's will. We often are so focused on our personal interpretation of His will that we ignore that much of His will is already laid out in His written word–truth. Since the Word (Logos) is spirit and life (John 6:63), the Word is Himself–truth. Because of His nature, He cannot violate Himself or His truth. Thus, as we seek God's will, we first must line up with the truth of the written Word and know that His specific will for us will encompass that truth and will not violate that truth.

John 14:1-6: He is TRUTH!

1 "Let not your heart be troubled; you believe in God, believe also in Me. 2 In My Father's house are many mansions; a if it were not so, I would have told you. I go to prepare a place for you. 3 And if I go and prepare a place for you, I will come again and receive you to Myself; that where I am, there you may be also. 4 And where I go you know, and the way you know." 5 Thomas said to Him, "Lord, we do not know where You are going, and how can we know the way?" 6 Jesus said to him, "I am the way, the truth, and the life. No one comes to the Father except through Me."

First, we must recognize that truth is not a set of principles, but rather a person–God Himself. He is the way, the life and the truth. Truth abides within Him and is absolute. There is no variation nor is it variable. Thus, we must fully recognize that His will is always in line with Himself–the way, the life and the truth. It will not compromise nor alter any of this truth.

2 Timothy 3:14-17: Holy Scripture is inspired (God breathed).

14 But you must continue in the things which you have learned and been assured of, knowing from whom you have learned them, 15 and that from childhood you have known the Holy Scriptures, which are able to make you wise for salvation through faith which is in Christ Jesus. 16 All Scripture is given by inspiration of God, and is profitable for doctrine, for reproof, for correction, for instruction in righteousness, 17 that the man of God may be complete, thoroughly equipped for every good work.

In order to experience God's will, we must hold a high view of Scripture. It is not just a history book or a set of principles, but rather is the very inspiring, living Word of God handed down to us. It is completely true in all aspects (both Old and New Testament), and all of it is to be considered as we receive and understand God's will. It is often referred to as the entire counsel of God—which gives truth and clarity to how we are to carry out our lives. The intention of the Word is to reveal to us doctrine—what is true for the grand and great life, and instruction—His specific will for us. The purpose is for us to be complete and equipped for every good work, which we learn from Ephesians 3:10 is already prepared in advance for us.

Scripture is profitable for us—that we will live out these truths, which will lead us to the grand plan that He has for us. Without considering the fundamental truths of Scripture, we will, by definition, miss His will for our life. Thus, it requires that we learn to abide in His word and to continue to deepen our relationship in truth, which will guide and direct our lives into His perfect will.

Romans 15:4:

4 For whatever things were written before were written for our learning, that we through the patience and comfort of the Scriptures might have hope.

Scripture is written specifically for our learning that, through persistent seeking of this wisdom, we might have great hope. Hope is not arbitrary, but geared toward the fulfillment of the great and abundant plan that God has for us.

Matthew 5:17-20: All that is truth is fulfilled in Christ–who fulfills all the Scripture (both OT and NT).

17 "Do not think that I came to destroy the Law or the Prophets. I did not come to destroy but to fulfill. 18 For assuredly, I say to you, till heaven and earth pass away, one jot or one tittle will by no means pass from the law till all is fulfilled. 19 Whoever therefore breaks one of the least of these commandments, and teaches men so, shall be called least in the kingdom of heaven; but whoever does and teaches them, he shall be called great in the kingdom of heaven. 20 For I say to you, that unless your righteousness exceeds the righteousness of the scribes and Pharisees, you will by no means enter the kingdom of heaven.

As stated above, all of Scripture is truth and this includes the Old and the New Testament. Many New Testament believers view the Old Testament as a history book, but not a truly valid tool for helping us to live out our lives today as Christians. Nothing could be further from the truth. It states specifically that Christ does not come to abolish the Old Testament truths, but to fulfill them completely. This is why it is so important to consider the whole counsel of God and all of the truths included in both the Old and New Testament. We are to receive instruction from both and let Him reveal to us the truth of both.

John 6:63, 68; 17:3: Spirit and Life; experiencing God in real life.

6:63 It is the Spirit who gives life; the flesh profits nothing. The words that I speak to you are spirit, and they are life

6:68 But Simon Peter answered Him, "Lord, to whom shall we go? You have the words of eternal life.

17:3 And this is eternal life, that they may know You, the only true God, and Jesus Christ whom You have sent.

The words from Scripture are Spirit and they are Life. (Word means: *life–real and genuine, a life active and vigorous, devoted to God, blessed, in the portion even in this world of those who put their trust in Christ.*) When you are abiding by the words being spoken to you by the Father through the Holy Spirit, they are more than concepts, ideas, principles, rules, etc.–rather, they are the essence of God transferring into us the very power and life of these words. They are active and stimulating–called quickening our hearts, which means: *by spiritual power to arouse and invigorate, to restore to life*–attractive to us, interesting, life giving.

Thus, if the words are the ones being spoken to us, they will have this quality–if there is life to us then we are to camp out there. If not, then do not strive to get something out of it–just move on to where there is life. If the Father needs us to receive something that we miss, we are not to worry–He will get us back there. These words are the words of eternal life, and Christ defines eternal life in John 17:3–knowing the Father and the Son. When? Now. Knowing is not knowing about or studying; rather, it is experiencing God in our everyday life. The Word means: *understand, perceive, have knowledge of, to understand.* How do we experience Him? Through His Life-giving, Spirit-filled words that He speaks to us–by abiding.

The Word is always where we will begin to discern His will. As we learn the processes of discernment we must commit to abiding in His Spirit and life words. Always and foremost go to His word to understand His truth, which will establish the foundation for His specific will for us. I urge you not to neglect how critical His word is to living out His will.

His will is not fuzzy about many things in our lives that have already been spelled out in Scripture, thus are we living in:

Forgiveness versus anger & revenge

Unity

Praise

Worship

Thankfulness

Enjoying work

Exceptional marriage

Servant

Humility

Integrity

Love

Peace

Joy

Kindness, tenderness

Respect

Patience

Freedom

Trust

Faith

Walking in the Spirit

Hearing His voice

Obeying

And then do we understand that many issues we face have already been spoken in Scripture, regarding how we are to live in dealing with situations such as:

Wronged by someone

Lawsuits

Guilt, past failures

Tithing

Saving

Get rich quick schemes

Marrying or partnering with unbelievers

Division

Parenting

Judgment

Addictions

Authority

Perseverance

Trials

As all these different scenarios enter our lives, our first thought should be to go to the Word and ask the Father if He has already addressed them. If He has, then we are to abide in that Word and receive the truth of exactly how it applies to us. It is not to be a mechanical law, but rather to stimulate a dialogue between the Father and us around this truth so that we can fully understand it and know how to apply it to our particular situation. We can trust that the outcome will be exactly as He planned because we are receiving instruction directly from Him, and following what He knows is best and none better. Why would we not?

5

HIS PLAN IS SPECIFIC FOR US
AND GIVEN TO US

As we discussed in the previous chapter, His will is based upon and is always subject to His written word. Interestingly enough, most believers have had a great misunderstanding on this point. Many do fully believe in the inerrancy and immutability of God's word (though lately more and more do not). However, they view this inerrant Word as a set of principles to which they are called to attempt to carry out. In other words, we wind up living our lives under law–trying to fulfill what we believe to be God's rules for living.

We then fail and get discouraged about the practicality of His word, and wonder why it seems impossible to carry out. What we need to fully understand is that His word is geared to provide the foundation for Him to communicate His specific will to us. It is to be given by Him and we are to receive it; it is to be unique and is a path that only we are given.

Proverbs 3:4-6: Direct our steps (specific):
4 And so find favor and high esteem In the sight of God and man. 5 Trust in the Lord with all your heart, And lean not on your own understanding; 6 In all your ways acknowledge Him, And He shall direct your paths.

This verse in Proverbs is very familiar to most of us. If we do not lean on our own understanding (which most of us actually do by default) and trust in God (which most of us do not do by default), then He will direct our steps. The Hebrew word for steps means that He will lead and direct us along a straight path which is very specific to us–and since walking down a path requires taking step-by-step, His will is given step-by-step. Thus, we must realize that He is the one directing and we are the ones to follow. If this is so, we must understand fully His directions so that we can follow exactly along the path—the steps He wishes us to take. It is specific and personal.

John 16:13-15: Guide, speak and reveal things to come along our steps.

13 However, when He, the Spirit of truth, has come, He will guide you into all truth; for He will not speak on His own authority, but whatever He hears He will speak; and He will tell you things to come. 14 He will glorify Me, for He will take of what is Mine and declare it to you. 15 All things that the Father has are Mine. Therefore I said that He will take of Mine and declare it to you.

Fortunately, we are not left to guess at His specific step-by-step will because we have His Holy Spirit residing within us. It is the Holy Spirit's specific job to guide us into His specific and personal will. He uses the precise word "guide" here for a reason. If any of us has experienced a tour guide, say at an art museum, we understand exactly what a guide does. What he does not do is take us to the cafeteria, give us a pamphlet (the Bible) and say, "read it, and I hope you fully understand it. Good luck; see you later." Rather the guide says, "Come with me." He takes us to a painting and begins to describe the truth of that painting. As we are curious and need more clarification, we ask questions. A good guide will spend lots of time answering those questions so that we fully understand and comprehend exactly what he wishes to reveal—the truth. And the good news is that the Holy Spirit is not restricting us to a one-hour tour—rather, He is infinitely patient for us to fully comprehend and receive His will with great clarity. He further tells us that He is to guide us into all truth. The word "truth" here does not mean just spiritual or God's truth, but literally all that is true.

Thus, as we are facing various circumstances and need to understand God's will, He will reveal to us the reality of all that is true, in all aspects of what is involved in the circumstances. For example, my wife Linda may have an understanding about something and engage me to help make a decision together. The truth at that moment is that I may be too stubborn to care, and thus try to sway the decision to my agenda. As Linda is walking in the Spirit, He will guide her to that truth and reveal to her where my heart really is, so that He can give her wisdom and clarity about how to bring me to a place of softness and surrender.

Thus, as we pursue God's will and are guided by the Holy Spirit, we are to have a passion for truth, what is real and how God is going to guide us through this reality. This further sets the stage for something we will discuss later: due diligence and seeking truth. As we make decisions and walk in God's will, we need to know what is real and what is true so that we don't assume something that will cause failure or lack of fulfillment of His will.

Another important role of the Holy Spirit is to tell us of things to come. As we are walking in His will, He knows what's around the corner. Often He needs to alert us to things coming that are going to impact the circumstances of His will and then how we are to be guided through them. This often involves alerting us to things to pay attention to.

For example, if I told you that tomorrow at the place where you are having lunch, a woman in a bright yellow dress was going to come up to your table and say something very significant to you, you would be watching for the woman in the yellow dress and pay attention to what she says. If I did not alert you, you would not know that this woman in the yellow dress is important, and probably not care about what she says. The Spirit is alerting you to what is ahead so you can hear more about where He wants to lead and guide you. Further, His job is to transfer all that is Christ's to you. Christ is living in the resurrection where all has been given Him. He wants to give us the abundant life here and now. The Holy Spirit is to be the transfer agent of this gift. All this happens through abiding.

Psalm 25:12: Teach the way. Psalm 32:8: Instruct and teach the way we are to go.

12 Who is the man that fears the Lord? Him shall He teach in the way He chooses.

37

We can rely on the promise of God that He will teach us the way that He chooses for us. It is His role to choose His specific will for us, and then to teach us to receive it and follow it. Teaching implies that it is a process. As we pursue God's will, He is not expecting us to simply comprehend it upon first disclosure, but rather to be an active learner in a teaching process. It means that we will be tested. For everything that we do not fully understand, He will work with us further to bring comprehension and clarity.

He is a gentle teacher who knows that we will either make mistakes or not quite get it. He is infinitely patient and only requires us to stay in the classroom—be a learner, stay with it, and grow in our under-standing as He teaches us the way that He has chosen for us. It is to be an enjoyable, very positive experience. He is not expecting perfection, but rather wants us to realize what a privilege it is to be taught. As He shows us the way, we are to pay attention, consider and ponder what it is that He is teaching. The word "teach" here means that He will point out, show, direct and instruct us in the specific path; since He sees all, He knows what is best and purposes to have us live out this best.

We had a young couple attend one of our living Waters spiritual retreats in Colorado. He was a financial adviser and she was an aspiring country music songwriter trying to break into the Nashville network. At the retreat, both expressed their frustration at being away from each other as she was traveling back and forth to Nashville and having no breakthrough. They wanted to settle into the city, buy a house (they currently owned a condo in Denver), and start a family. At the retreat, they learned to hear from God and that God had a specific plan, espe-cially for them. So they began to pray and ask for insight and wisdom regarding God's will for all these questions. They heard to continue to try to break into Nashville, and that God would make things clear to them. They trusted what they were hearing and followed God's direc-tion, step-by-step.

Within six months, she had made a connection in Nashville, but re-ceived a larger contract in broader music venues from an international company headquartered in Los Angeles. This new company commit-ted to limit her travel and would allow her to build her marriage and start a family. They were led by God to sell their condo and received top price in a down market. They moved to Southern California and have had a beautiful life together. He has built his financial advising company and she has several hit songs. They are now starting a family. When they released all the decisions to God, surrendered to His will, and expected to hear His will, all the pressure was off of them, and they stopped trying to figure things out on their own, as well as trying to make things happen on their own. Rather, they have experienced the sweet joy of following God into His grand plan for them.

6

JESUS LAYS OUT HIS PROCESS IN HIS UPPER ROOM PRAYER TO THE FATHER BEFORE HE MARCHES TO THE CROSS AND RESURRECTION

John 17:

1 Jesus spoke these words, lifted up His eyes to heaven, and said: "Father, the hour has come. Glorify Your Son, that Your Son also may glorify You, 2 as You have given Him authority over all flesh, that He should give eternal life to as many as You have given Him. 3 And this is eternal life, that they may know You, the only true God, and Jesus Christ whom You have sent. 4 I have glorified You on the earth. I have finished the work which You have given Me to do. 5 And now, O Father, glorify Me together with Yourself, with the glory which I had with You before the world was. 6 "I have manifested Your name to the men whom You have given Me out of the world. They were Yours, You gave them to Me, and they have kept Your word. 7 Now they have known that all things which You have given Me are from You. 8 For I have given to them the words which You have given Me; and they have received them, and have known surely that I came forth from You; and they have believed that You sent Me. 9 I pray for them. I do not pray for the world but for those whom You have given Me, for they are Yours. 10 And all Mine are Yours, and Yours are Mine, and I am glorified in them. 11 Now I am no longer in the world, but these are in the world, and I come to You. Holy Father, keep through Your name those whom You have given Me, that they may be one as We are. 12 While I was with them in the world, I kept them in Your name. Those whom You gave Me I have kept; and none of them is lost except the son of perdition, that the Scripture might be fulfilled. 13 But now I come to You, and these things I speak in the world, that they may have My joy fulfilled in themselves. 14 I have given them Your word; and the world has hated them because they are not of the world, just as I am not of the world. 15 I do not pray that You should take them out of the world, but that You should keep them from the evil one. 16 They are not of the world, just as I am not of the world. 17 Sanctify them by Your truth. Your word is truth. 18 As You sent Me into the world, I also have sent them into the world. 19 And for their sakes I sanctify Myself, that they also may be sanctified by the truth. 20 "I do not pray for these alone, but also for those who will believe in Me through their word; 21 that they all may be one, as You, Father, are in Me, and I in You; that they also may be one in Us, that the world may believe that You sent Me. 22 And the glory which You gave Me I have given them, that they may be one just as We are one: 23 I in them, and You in Me; that they may be made perfect in one, and that the world may know that You have sent Me, and have loved them as You have loved Me. 24 Father, I desire that they also, whom You gave Me may be with Me where I am, that they may behold My glory which You have given Me; for You loved Me before the foundation of the world. 25 O righteous Father! The world has not known You, but I have known You; and these have known that You sent Me. 26 And I have declared to them Your name, and will declare it, that the love with which You loved Me may be in them, and I in them."

After Jesus had given His most powerful series of messages to His disciples in the upper room, He laid out His prayer for His disciples and all His followers thereafter (including us). This prayer gives the specifics of His will and how we are to join His will.

17:1-2: First, He states that all authority is being handed over to Him. The word "authority" means: *the ability or strength with which one is endued, which he either possesses or exercises, the power of authority (influence) and of right (privilege), the power of rule or government (the power of him whose will and commands must be submitted to by others and obeyed).* In order for us to experience His will, we must recognize and submit to His "Ruler-ship." He is King of His kingdom, and thus His will is found in His kingdom under His authority. Further, His will involves His authority–it is not a natural, intellectual way of life, but rather a supernatural way of life that is to experience His supreme authority over both the physical and the spiritual realms.

17:3: His purpose of His will is for us to experience, in a real way, the life of the Father and of the Son. Eternal life is not a transaction that moves us to heaven when we die, but rather starts when we submit to His will. His will is to get to know the character, purposes, ways and miraculous power of the Father and of the Son.

17:4-5: He sets the promise of how His will is to be carried out–to complete the work of the Father. Thus, we are to be occupied in our everyday life with His will–what is His specific plan? For us, it will include the what, the when and the how; as it did for Christ who only did what the Father gave Him as His will.

17:6-19: He then goes on to give us the purpose of joining His will–to manifest His name to those around us. The word "manifest" means: *make manifest or visible or known what has been hidden or unknown;* and His "name" means: *the name is used for everything which the name covers, everything the thought or feeling of which is aroused in the mind by mentioning, hearing, remembering, the name, (i.e. for one's rank, authority, interests, pleasure, command, excellences, deeds).* His will is to bring glory to Himself and that, through our day-to-day lives, we will show the world the full character and power of God–His name, which is all aspects of His character and power. Progressively, we are to receive and display this character in reality–not philosophically or theologically, but truly reflecting God in us.

His will is carried out by keeping His word–given to us to be received and believed. We are to attend to His word carefully, realize that He is giving His word to us specifically, and then we are to receive it by taking it as our own and living it out. In these verses, Christ uses both Logos (written Word) and Rhema (personal Spirit Word to us). Rhema means that the promise and truth written for mankind through His Bible (Logos) is now spoken and given specifically to me personally–it applies to my circumstances and my particular time.

As we glorify Him through following His will we will experience many beautiful truths in our lives:

♦ ***We will be One with the Father and the Son–when we are walking in His will through the Holy Spirit.***

♦ *We will experience great joy through receiving what He speaks (His exceptional will).*

♦ *We will experience His word (logos) not in a bubble exempt from trouble; but to be carried out in enemy territory—the world that is Satan's kingdom and domain.*

♦ *We will be kept from the evil one. His will for us is to not function in kingdom of enemy but in God's kingdom.*

♦ *We will be sanctified (purified) by truth: the word truth here is not relegated to just spiritual truth, but rather all truth. What is true in any matter under consideration; truly, in truth, according to truth; of a truth, in reality, in fact, certainly which then leads us to the Word (Logos)—revealing how to live this out through instruction for the good work already prepared.*

17:20-26: He then concludes His prayer as He lays out His prescription for us joining His will by summarizing the purpose for us to join His will:

♦ *Oneness—that the world may believe in the reality of God and that His power through and for us is real, to be trusted and experienced.*

♦ *We are to become whole (salvation: healed, delivered and living the abundant life) and that the world will know to whom we belong—children of the almighty God.*

♦ *We are to be with Him (in the Resurrection and living in the Resurrection power); that we will experience the Father's love in us; and our entire life is intended to declare His name.*

Linda and I can attest to the wonder of this process being real, and experiencing the oneness and joy of walking in the Spirit since we are walking in His will, which is best and none better. This even applies when we are being challenged to go deeper and grow in our inadequacies and limitations. Living in Colorado, Linda and I often get into the car and drive up into the mountains to go for a hike together. When we do, we bring our Bibles and our journals and share what God is speaking to us. I was in a particular passage in Luke in my "abiding," so I had Linda read the verses from Luke. As she did, one of the verses quickened my spirit and caught my attention. I asked her to cross reference that particular verse. It led to Malachi, which is God's message to repent from living a life that is not of God. He said to have Linda read the entire book (fortunately, which is short).

I asked the Father if he was unhappy with me, wondering if I had drifted away from Him. He said no, but that He just wanted to take us deeper, to a higher level of spirituality and to use Malachi as the platform. Over the next six months, I camped out in the book of Malachi, verse by verse, and was led to the beauty of not living at a level of spiritual satisfaction, but rather being challenged to go to a much higher and much deeper place. God loves us too much to actually leave us alone. He is always drawing us to a greater level of amazement, joy and wonder with Him. Even as I was personally convicted to the study of Malachi, I experienced the fullness of oneness, his joy, and the beautiful transformation that He did inside of me. I experienced His word on a much more personal level, and allowed Him to sanctify me in the process. It was a terrific journey.

7
HOW DO WE DISCERN THIS PLAN
(HIS WILL)?

It begins with and always depends upon our surrender of our will to His will:

Mark 1:14-18:
14 Now after John was put in prison, Jesus came to Galilee, preaching the gospel of the kingdom of God, 15 and saying, "The time is fulfilled, and the kingdom of God is at hand. Repent, and believe in the Gospel." 16 And as He walked by the Sea of Galilee, He saw Simon and Andrew his brother casting a net into the sea; for they were fishermen. 17 Then Jesus said to them, "Follow Me, and I will make you become fishers of men." 18 They immediately left their nets and followed Him.

Jesus first calls all of us to repent and live in His kingdom. "Repentance" means to turn around–to turn from self and follow Him (The Person Christ and His will), as He draws us into His bigger story to be made fishers of men. We are to surrender to His royal power, His kingship, His dominion and His rule, as we fully believe by being persuaded that His will is best and none better.

Deuteronomy 30:11-20: Life/death; blessing/cursing; choose His way or not.
11 "For this commandment which I command you today is not too mysterious for you, nor is it far off. 12 It is not in heaven, that you should say, 'Who will ascend into heaven for us and bring it to us, that we may hear it and do it?' 13 Nor is it beyond the sea, that you should say, 'Who will go over the sea for us and bring it to us, that we may hear it and do it?' 14 But the word is very near you, in your mouth and in your heart, that you may do it. 15 "See, I have set before you today life and good, death and evil, 16 in that I command you today to love the Lord your God, to walk in His

45

ways, and to keep His commandments, His statutes, and His judgments, that you may live and multiply; and the Lord your God will bless you in the land which you go to possess. 17 But if your heart turns away so that you do not hear, and are drawn away, and worship other gods and serve them, 18 I announce to you today that you shall surely perish; you shall not prolong your days in the land which you cross over the Jordan to go in and possess. 19 I call heaven and earth as witnesses today against you, that I have set before you life and death, blessing and cursing; therefore choose life, that both you and your descendants may live; 20 that you may love the Lord your God, that you may obey His voice, and that you may cling to Him, for He is your life and the length of your days; and that you may dwell in the land which the Lord swore to your fathers, to Abraham, Isaac, and Jacob, to give them."

In Deuteronomy 28 through 30, God reveals great detail about His covenant to us–that we are to be blessed to become a blessing. However, He makes it clear that our experiencing this covenant is dependent upon a fundamental choice of surrender that we must make. God sets before us a blessing and a curse. He further states that receiving His instruction through His word is not too difficult–we are called to read and interpret Scripture simply, and that it is the Holy Spirit's job to bring revelation of His Scripture to us in a way that we can understand. It requires no special skills, and we do not need someone else (especially those we consider more spiritually mature) to give us answers–we can receive them directly from God! Then, God presents to us the clarity of a blessing and a curse.

The Word is a double-edged sword; if we follow and are obedient to what God is instructing us, we will receive the promised blessing. If we choose not to follow and obey His instructions (His will), we walk into the curse and the negative effects and consequences of that curse by being disobedient. The word "evil" here does not mean satanic or "black," but rather: full of labors, annoyances, hardships; pressed and harassed; bringing toils, annoyances, perils; of a time full of peril to Christian faith and steadfastness; causing pain and trouble; bad, of a bad nature or condition; in a physical sense: diseased or blind. Basically, we will be experiencing the life of Satan's kingdom, which is to kill, steal and destroy. This is why His setting forth blessing and cursing is so simple–if we follow His will, we will avoid the continual life of difficulty and experience His blessed abundant life. Remember, this does not mean that we will not experience trouble, as we live in enemy territory, but rather trouble will not dominate us and characterize our everyday life. We are to live in the spectacular will of the Father–which is best and none better. And why does He lay out this clear and simple choice?

We have a tendency to believe that disobedience means doing awful things. Rather, it is simply not following completely the instructions God is setting for us. He also brings clarity in that He makes it clear the blessing and the benefit being offered, versus the awful consequences if we choose not to follow. Please note that if we aren't hearing His voice, it is because our hearts have turned away–basically that we have chosen to walk our own way and not truly surrender and follow Him and His will. As a result, we stop hearing His voice and enter into a time of confusion.

The resolution to this dilemma is to confess and then return by desiring to walk with Him. This stimulates our ability to hear His voice, and thus hear His instructions. God desires us to choose life by choosing Him. Because it is a choice, we either will suffer the consequences or enjoy the blessings of our choices. We know that the very fundamental choice is to abide–because as John 15: 5 says, "Apart from Me you can do nothing." So abiding is a critical choice that everyone must make every day. That is where we will be in relationship to God, hearing His voice and being able to follow His ways by walking with Him.

1 Samuel 12:14-15:

14 If you fear the Lord and serve Him and obey His voice, and do not rebel against the commandment of the Lord, then both you and the king who reigns over you will continue following the Lord your God. 15 However, if you do not obey the voice of the Lord, but rebel against the commandment of the Lord, then the hand of the Lord will be against you, as it was against your fathers.

Here, God makes another significant statement: If we continue (not once but always) to follow His will by serving Him and obeying His voice, we will experience His best. If we do not follow the voice of the Lord, and thus rebel against His instruction, the very hand of God will come against us. It is so simple—in addition to experiencing the difficulty of the world by being outside of God's will, our specific choice of not desiring to follow His will brings God's activity against us—it will not go well for us. Why anyone would not choose to follow God's will is beyond me. It just does not make sense. We must remember that the only purpose of God working against us is to cause us to repent. Basically, He is asking us a very simple question: How is that going for you? Since it will not be going well, He wants us to realize that we are to repent and turn around and seek His will. Why would we not?

John 5:18-20, 30; John 8:28-30:

John 5:18 Therefore the Jews sought all the more to kill Him, because He had not only broken the Sabbath, but also said that God was His Father, making Himself equal with God. 19 Then Jesus answered and said to them, "Most assuredly, I say to you, the Son can do nothing of Himself, but what He sees the Father do; for whatever He does, the Son also does in like manner. 20 For the Father loves the Son, and shows Him all things that He Himself does; and He will show Him greater works than these, that you may marvel.

John 5:30 I can of Myself do nothing. As I hear, I judge; and My judgment is righteous, because I do not seek My own will but the will of the Father who sent Me.

John 8:28-30 Then Jesus said to them, "When you lift up the Son of Man, then you will know that I am He, and that I do nothing of Myself; but as My Father taught Me, I speak these things. 29 And He who sent Me is with Me. The Father has not left Me alone, for I always do those things that please Him." 30 As He spoke these words, many believed in Him.

He further punctuates this point for us by stating that Jesus Christ, His son, only operated in His will. He only walked where the Father was at work and only carried out what was spoken to Him. He only did what pleased the Father. We must realize the power of the words used here by Christ. The word "nothing" means nil, zero, zip. It means that it was not just operational sometimes, but rather He did absolutely nothing that was outside of God's will. And His will was not generic, but was rather specific, step-by-step, day-by-day as Christ carried it out.

John 15:5:

Having made this amazing statement that He did nothing except what was given by the Father, He then brings us to the same place. Apart from Him we can do nothing–nil, zero, zip. This is a statement that we must fully absorb and realize its impact. Most Christians are doing things that they believe are working for God–lots of ministry, good works, benevolence, etc. However, if they are being carried out outside of God's will, apart from Him, they are amounting to nothing– because it is not where God is at work, but rather where we are at work in the natural. If we truly believed this, we would abide in Him, and we would only desire to do His will, day-by-day, step-by-step.

Examples:
In the Gospel, we have great examples of how this concept worked, illustrating that Christ did only what the Father spoke.

John 2:1-12:
1 On the third day there was a wedding in Cana of Galilee, and the mother of Jesus was there. 2 Now both Jesus and His disciples were invited to the wedding. 3 And when they ran out of wine, the mother of Jesus said to Him, "They have no wine." 4 Jesus said to her, "Woman, what does your concern have to do with Me? My hour has not yet come." 5 His mother said to the servants, "Whatever He says to you, do it." 6 Now there were set there six waterpots of stone, according to the manner of purification of the Jews,

49

containing twenty or thirty gallons apiece. 7 Jesus said to them, "Fill the waterpots with water." And they filled them up to the brim. 8 And He said to them, "Draw some out now, and take it to the master of the feast." And they took it. 9 When the master of the feast had tasted the water that was made wine, and did not know where it came from (but the servants who had drawn the water knew), the master of the feast called the bridegroom. 10 And he said to him, "Every man at the beginning sets out the good wine, and when the guests have well drunk, then the inferior. You have kept the good wine until now!" 11 This beginning of signs Jesus did in Cana of Galilee, and manifested His glory; and His disciples believed in Him. 12 After this He went down to Capernaum, He, His mother, His brothers, and His disciples; and they did not stay there many days.

Jesus' first miracle was turning water into wine. He and His family attended a wedding feast in Cana, about a day's walk from Nazareth. Jewish weddings were a tremendous celebration. They would last several days up to a week, and the guest's wedding present to the bride and groom was food—in the same vein as current day Christian potlucks. They would bring food for themselves and/or others so that everyone would be sufficiently fed for an entire week.

The father of the bridegroom was responsible for the wine for the entire group for the entire week. It was real wine (not grape juice) and was typically drunk by everyone of that era. It was alcoholic by definition but would have been a lower alcohol content then our current wine offerings. When Mary, Jesus' mother, noticed that they had run out of wine, she told Jesus to take care of it. Think for a moment the source of this request—she was not asking Him to go buy more wine, but rather to perform a miracle by turning water into wine. On what basis could she have asked this? Because He had done it at home many times before.

Since age 12, Jesus understood that He was about His Father's business and was the Messiah. At home for 18 years, He had practiced following the will of the Father and performing supernatural acts. He had already turned water into wine. Upon hearing His mother's request,

He stated that it was not yet His time to do miracles publicly. She turned to the servants and said to do whatever He asked. She understood that, yes, it was His time.

Between hearing His mother and His initial response, Jesus checked in with the Father and asked Him specifically if this was His time. The Father said "yes." Jesus, having heard His will, was immediately obedient and turned the water into wine. How do we know this to be so? Because He stated in John 5 that He did nothing except what He heard from the Father. Since He performed this miracle having first stated that He thought it was not yet His time, He surrendered His will to the Father and performed the miracle.

It was a spectacular miracle as 180+ gallons of water were turned into wine, and the guests were overwhelmed at how special this wine was compared to what they had already drunk. It is customary to bring out weaker wine to make it last longer as the celebration dragged on. Interestingly enough, the first ones that realized that this was miraculous were the servants. This whole story illustrates that Jesus receives specific instructions from the Father and He willingly carried them out. It is also important to note that this instruction was initiated by His mother–so we are not to develop a system for how we hear the Father's will–rather just to be open to Him communicating His will to us through numerous means; but we will still know it is Him.

Luke 19:1-10:
1 Then Jesus entered and passed through Jericho. 2 Now behold, there was a man named Zacchaeus who was a chief tax collector, and he was rich. 3 And he sought to see who Jesus was, but could not because of the crowd, for he was of short stature. 4 So he ran ahead and climbed up into a sycamore tree to see Him, for He was going to pass that way. 5 And when Jesus came to the place, He looked up and saw him, and said to him, "Zacchaeus, make haste and come down, for today I must stay at your house." 6 So he made haste and came down, and received Him joyfully. 7 But when they saw it, they all complained, saying, "He has gone to be a guest with a man who is a sinner." 8 Then Zacchaeus stood and said to the Lord, "Look, Lord, I give half of my goods to the poor; and if I have taken anything from

anyone by false accusation, I restore fourfold." 9 And Jesus said to him, "To-day salvation has come to this house, because he also is a son of Abraham; 10 for the Son of Man has come to seek and to save that which was lost."

In this story from Luke, Jesus meets Zacchaeus. He is on His way to Jerusalem to enter the city on what we call Palm Sunday. He's being hailed as a king–the Messiah King–which is why people were laying palm branches down before Him. On route to Jerusalem, He passes through Jericho where people are also lining up, hailing Him as Messiah King. Amongst this crowd is a short man who climbs up in a tree and shouts out Jesus' name. Jesus stops and goes over to him and makes an incredible statement, "Zacchaeus, come down for I MUST spend the day with you." Why would He make such a declarative statement? Because He heard the Father say to stop and spend the day with Zacchaeus.

He had not planned on stopping anywhere in Jericho, other than to pass through on His way to Jerusalem. His daily plan was altered because it was God's will that He spend the day with Zacchaeus and responding to Zacchaeus' attempt to get Jesus' attention. It is likely that, on many occasions, people shouted out His name but He did not specifically stop to spend the day with them. In this situation He did because, again, He only did what the Father spoke, and the Father spoke that it was His will for Jesus to spend a full day with this person.

These examples illustrate that the Father has a will, which is very specific, and is able to communicate that will to those who are willing and able to hear.

Our Choice:

John 4:34; 6:38; Mark 14:32-42:
John 4:34 Jesus said to them, "My food is to do the will of Him who sent Me, and to finish His work.

John 6:38 For I have come down from heaven, not to do My own will, but the will of Him who sent Me.

Mark 14:32 Then they came to a place, which was named Gethsemane; and He said to His disciples, "Sit here while I pray." 33 And He took Peter, James, and John with Him, and He began to be troubled and deeply distressed. 34 Then He said to them, "My soul is exceedingly sorrowful, even to death. Stay here and watch." 35 He went a little farther, and fell on the ground, and prayed that if it were possible, the hour might pass from Him. 36 And He said, "Abba, Father, all things are possible for You. Take this cup away from Me; nevertheless, not what I will, but what You will." 37 Then He came and found them sleeping, and said to Peter, "Simon, are you sleeping? Could you not watch one hour? 38 Watch and pray, lest you enter into temptation. The spirit indeed is willing, but the flesh is weak." 39 Again He went away and prayed, and spoke the same words. 40 And when He returned, He found them asleep again, for their eyes were heavy; and they did not know what to answer Him. 41 Then He came the third time and said to them, "Are you still sleeping and resting? It is enough! The hour has come; behold, the Son of Man is being betrayed into the hands of sinners. 42 Rise, let us be going. See, My betrayer is at hand."

As we choose to repent and live in His kingdom, choose blessing and life rather than cursing and death, and realize that apart from Him we can do nothing (as Christ understood with the Father); we must have a heart like Christ's who only came to do the will of the Father. Throughout His ministry, it is recorded that He had no difficulty with hearing, receiving, and then following completely the Father's will—in everything.

However, He did go through an extreme test in the Garden of Gethsemane. Facing His march to the crucifixion, He became very sorrowful—so overcome with sadness that it alone almost caused His death. Having understood the nature and sovereignty of God, He appealed to the Father to please come up with an alternative plan. Jesus knew that nothing was impossible for the Father. He knew that the Father had the power to come up with a different plan and asked Him to take away the cup before Him. His answer was, "No, this is the only way that I have chosen and is My will." He exits the garden once and states, "Not My will be done but Yours."

Why, then, did He go back a second time? Because Jesus knew that, though He intellectually assented to following God's will, He did not have it settled in His heart (soul). So He struggled through a second time with the same question to the Father, only to emerge from the garden again with His statement that, "Not My will but Thine be done." Why, then, did He return a third time? Same reason. Intellectually He assented, but knew in His heart that it was not settled. It was not until the third time (which was after many hours of battle in the garden) did He emerge with it settled in His heart. From this point, following through to the crucifixion, there was no more struggle or difficulty with following His will. It truly was settled.

Since we are engaged in a daily battle of flesh (self) versus the Spirit, we have to constantly go through our own Gethsemane until we emerge with it settled in our heart–not my will but Thine be done.

Matthew 16:13-28:

13 When Jesus came into the region of Caesarea Philippi, He asked His disciples, saying, "Who do men say that I, the Son of Man, am?" 14 So they said, "Some say John the Baptist, some Elijah, and others Jeremiah or one of the prophets." 15 He said to them, "But who do you say that I am?" 16 Simon Peter answered and said, "You are the Christ, the Son of the living God." 17 Jesus answered and said to him, "Blessed are you, Simon Bar-Jonah, for flesh and blood has not revealed this to you, but My Father who is in heaven. 18 And I also say to you that you are Peter, and on this rock I will build My church, and the gates of Hades shall not prevail against it. 19 And I will give you the keys of the kingdom of heaven, and whatever you bind on earth will be bound in heaven, and whatever you loose on earth will be loosed in heaven." 20 Then He commanded His disciples that they should tell no one that He was Jesus the Christ. 21 From that time Jesus began to show to His disciples that He must go to Jerusalem, and suffer many things from the elders and chief priests and scribes, and be killed, and be raised the third day. 22 Then Peter took Him aside and began to rebuke

Him, saying, "Far be it from You, Lord; this shall not happen to You!" 23 But He turned and said to Peter, "Get behind Me, Satan! You are an offense to Me, for you are not mindful of the things of God, but the things of men." 24 Then Jesus said to His disciples, "If anyone desires to come after Me, let him deny himself, and take up his cross, and follow Me. 25 For whoever desires to save his life will lose it, but whoever loses his life for My sake will find it. 26 For what profit is it to a man if he gains the whole world, and loses his own soul? Or what will a man give in exchange for his soul? 27 For the Son of Man will come in the glory of His Father with His angels, and then He will reward each according to his works. 28 Assuredly, I say to you, there are some standing here who shall not taste death till they see the Son of Man coming in His kingdom

Denying self will is a daily battle (every single day). This cannot just be an intellectual assent–which most of us can say–but rather a true battle of the soul until we fully commit to following His will. Just as it was for Christ, there is no other way, Our own "Gethsemane" is required in order for us to choose life and blessing. I urge you not to neglect this critical step, and do not give it just a short intellectual assent. Battle through until you fully have a heart to follow God's will.

Fortunately, we do not have to go through the crucifixion too. Rather, we just have to deny self (surrender our will), stand on what Christ has already completed at the cross by fully understanding the defeat of Satan and the forgiveness given, and then follow Him and His will day by day. Christ is living in the resurrection where He wants us to live. We are to follow Him to where His amazing power can deliver to us the supernatural, abundant life. Daily deny self, take up your cross, and follow Him. It is so profound and simple, yet it does require a constant battling of our will in our personal Gethsemane and then choosing to follow Him.

Acts 13:16-23; Psalm 40:6-8; Hebrews 10:5-10:

Acts 13:16 Then Paul stood up, and motioning with his hand said, "Men of Israel, and you who fear God, listen: 17 The God of this people Israel chose our fathers, and exalted the people when they dwelt as strangers in the land of Egypt, and with an uplifted arm He brought them out of it. 18 Now for a time of about forty years He put up with their ways in the wilderness. 19 And when He had destroyed seven nations in the land of Canaan, He distributed their land to them by allotment. 20 After that He gave them judges for about four hundred and fifty years, until Samuel the prophet. 21 And afterward they asked for a king; so God gave them Saul the son of Kish, a man of the tribe of Benjamin, for forty years. 22 And when He had removed him, He raised up for them David as king, to whom also He gave testimony and said, 'I have found David the son of Jesse, a man after My own heart, who will do all My will.' 23 From this man's seed, according to the promise, God raised up for Israel a Savior, Jesus.

Psalm 40:6 Sacrifice and offering You did not desire; My ears You have opened. Burnt offering and sin offering You did not require. 7 Then I said, "Behold, I come; In the scroll of the book it is written of me. 8 I delight to do Your will, O my God, And Your law is within my heart."

Hebrews 10:5 Therefore, when He came into the world, He said: "Sacrifice and offering You did not desire, But a body You have prepared for Me. 6 In burnt offerings and sacrifices for sin You had no pleasure. 7 Then I said, 'Behold, I have come—In the volume of the book it is written of Me—To do Your will, O God.' 8 Previously saying, "Sacrifice and offering, burnt offerings, and offerings for sin You did not desire, nor had pleasure in them" (which are offered according to the law), 9 then He said, "Behold, I have come to do Your will, O God." He takes away the first that He may establish the second. 10 By that will we have been sanctified through the offering of the body of Jesus Christ once for all.

Another great example in Scripture is Paul's statement in Acts 13 about David. This section is the most concise history of Israel that exists in Scripture. It primarily talks about each era of Israel's history as he is presenting the importance of that history to the death and resurrection of Christ. However, in the middle of this brief description, he specifically names David and says that he was a man after God's own heart because he desired to do all of God's will.

We know that David was not perfect, and often made choices that were not of God. So how could it be said that he desired to do all of God's will? Because, in the depth of his soul, he did and when confronted with poor choices, he repented and went back again to following God's will. This is one of the most important questions that we have to answer—do we have a heart to follow all of God's will?

I urge you to reflect on this question: Can this truly be said of you? If not, then perhaps reread this chapter and reflect on the choices that we must make in our personal battles in order to come to the same place that David did. Psalm 40 states that: it was written that David delighted to do only God's will, and that His law or instruction was within His heart. (Please note that receiving God's instruction, particularly from His written Word, requires abiding, which we will discuss again in chapter 8.) Another question to you: Do you delight to do God's will and is His instruction in your heart? The same verses are attributed to Christ in Hebrews 10—that He delighted to do His will, even going to His death.

As we can see from these verses, doing God's will starts in the heart. Are we choosing to repent and live in His kingdom? Are we choosing blessing and life instead of death and cursing? Are we understanding that apart from Christ we can do nothing, in the same way Christ related to the Father? Are we willing to go through a personal Gethsemane to surrender our will until we delight to do His will, and it can be said of us that we are a person after God's own heart because we desire to do all of His will? It is important to note that hearing, receiving, understanding and then being able to follow God's will is not a mechanical process, but is rather a spiritual process of the heart. It starts with deciding, "Am I surrendered to that will?"

A couple with kids in college attended one of our retreats. The husband was a seminary graduate and they had been active in ministry, as well as had a management job with a Fortune 500 company. They both struggled with the concept of "abiding" and hearing from God. After the retreat, they invited us to dinner and shared that they were struggling in their marriage and considering separation. We walked them through the verses of this chapter and laid it at their feet—were they willing to surrender their will to God, who would restore their marriage and bring them in abundant life? (Remember, abundance is not wealth, but rather the wonder and joy of the fullness of God's life for us.)

They both were willing to meditate on these verses and then ponder their responses. As they spent time in these verses ("abiding"), they both heard from God that He was going to restore their marriage, their finances (struggling in bankruptcy) and their family.

So, when we met again, they said that they had chosen life and were surrendering their will to God, seeking His will and expecting His promise of restoration to be real. This couple is a shining example of how beautifully this choice means the difference between blessing and cursing—life and death. Their finances have been restored, their marriage is truly exceptional, and their family is all experiencing the joy of hearing from God, and each of their children walking into the exceptional will of God themselves.

This couple is now teaching about "abiding" and have multiplied what they have learned many-fold. In our ministry, Linda and I realize how beautiful it is to "give it away," as it has nothing to do with us, but rather is God's work. We, per se, have nothing to say and understand that our role is to help others get connected to the Vine, begin hearing from God, surrender their will, and discover God's unique will for them. It is truly a joy to behold.

8

BEING ABLE TO FOLLOW HIS WILL IS ALWAYS BASED UPON OUR ABIDING AND LIVING OUT HIS TRUTH ALREADY REVEALED–BEING TRANSFORMED INTO THE IMAGE OF CHRIST

John 8:28-36:

28 Then Jesus said to them, "When you lift up the Son of Man, then you will know that I am He, and that I do nothing of Myself; but as My Father taught Me, I speak these things. 29 And He who sent Me is with Me. The Father has not left Me alone, for I always do those things that please Him. 30 As He spoke these words, many believed in Him. 31 Then Jesus said to those Jews who believed Him, "If you abide in My word, you are My disciples indeed. 32 And you shall know the truth, and the truth shall make you free." 33 They answered Him, "We are Abraham's descendants, and have never been in bondage to anyone. How can you say, 'You will be made free'?" 34 Jesus answered them, "Most assuredly, I say to you, whoever commits sin is a slave of sin. 35 And a slave does not abide in the house forever, but a son abides forever. 36 Therefore if the Son makes you free, you shall be free indeed.

Jesus follows His statement that He only has done what the Father has spoken with an amazing truth: If we abide in His word we will know the truth, and the truth will set us free. The key aspect of truth for us personally is the fullness of God's will, and it is based upon abiding. Abiding leads to TRUTH, which leads to FREEDOM. Truth means all truth. Not just theological truth, but the truth about my situation and circumstances, the truth of my heart, the truth of my emotions and the truth that He desires for us to understand and receive His will.

Thus, we are called to develop two passions–abiding and truth. We are to abide in HIM–all the time–not just a few minutes before we go to work or on Sundays. As we actively pursue and enjoy abiding, we then are to develop a passion for truth. To stay "camped" out in His word until we understand, receive, believe and are obedient to the truth.

We do not accept something just because we can read it, hear a sermon or message on it, or read a commentary on it. No, we are to stay abiding ourselves in His word and in intimacy with Him until the truth is known and resonates in our heart (our soul). The Spirit is to continue to cause us to be unsettled, until the truth is His truth settled within our heart. This, then, drives us to stay abiding until the truth is known and received. Not striving or working on our part–rather, the joy of the relationship as He walks us into the truth. What a privilege!

The promised outcome is freedom; the word here means liberty, release. Not caught up in bondage or restriction, but rather set free to enjoy the abundant life He promises to deliver to us. To freely receive and live out His abundant, fantastic will. Wow!

This is not to be an arduous nor complicated process, but rather a beautiful walk, connected to the Vine. We should be relaxed, free from anxiety and fear, not thinking so much about outcomes and what may happen (particularly the negative). We should enjoy the rest, peace, good pace and margin in our life, while participating in giving it away to others and seeing the joy of transformation as others get connected to the Vine. It comes to us as His promise to us–IF we abide in His word, we WILL know the TRUTH, and the TRUTH will set us FREE. Let's look specifically at what Christ says about abiding:

John 15:1-5; 7-8:
1 "I am the true vine, and My Father is the vinedresser. 2 Every branch in Me that does not bear fruit He takes away; and every branch that bears fruit He prunes, that it may bear more fruit. 3 You are already clean because of the word which I have spoken to you. 4 Abide in Me, and I in you. As the branch cannot bear fruit of itself, unless it abides in the vine, neither can you, unless you abide in Me. 5 I am the vine, you are the branches. He

*who abides in Me, and I in him, bears much fruit; for without Me you can
do nothing... 7 If you abide in Me, and My words abide in you, you will
ask for what you desire, and it shall be done for you. 8 By this My Father is
glorified, that you bear much fruit; so you will be My disciples.*

Jesus lays out a beautiful analogy–the operation of the vineyard.
Interestingly, this analogy still holds true today. The process of growing
grapes and making wine is really the same as it was in Jesus' day (other
than newer technology for measuring things like water, humidity etc.,
but the process is still an art and not a mechanical science). He lays out
for us the important players in this process and the process itself:

♦ **The Vine–Christ.** The Vine is the source of life. Christ
   Himself is the Vine–the source of life (the good, abundant
   life).

♦ **The Vinedresser–The Father.** He makes all decisions of
   the vineyard (which grapes to grow, how much to water
   the soil, when to harvest, when to prune etc.). The Father
   makes all the decisions for our life as well–His will. It is
   what I call, directing all traffic in our life. He has already
   planned out in great detail what the abundant life looks
   like for each of us and how He wants to deliver this to us.
   The Vinedresser is the one who takes care of all issues–and
   no one else (especially us). He has a specific will and desires to carry out His will in our lives.

♦ **The Branches–Us.** We are branches. Branches just need
   to stay connected and not much else. We are not to attempt to be the Vine and especially not the Vinedresser.
   We are incapable of creating our own abundant life. He
   has to deliver it to us. Surrendering our will and experiencing His will demands us to just be a branch.

- **The Sap (Implied)–The Holy Spirit.** The Holy Spirit flows from the life of the Vine into and through the branches to the fruit. The Spirit is the Holy Spirit, and is God, within God the Father and God the Son and also within us. This life is intended to flow from the Vinedresser, through the Vine, through the branches and into the fruit. The only way to experience the life of the Spirit is to be connected, to truly be a branch to the Vine. This requires abiding.

- **The Result–Fruit: More Fruit: Much Fruit.** The vinedresser actually cares deeply about this–the overall objective of the vineyard–to have fruit that remains and fulfills the purposes of the Vinedresser.

- **The Choice–Abide.** Our choice. He does not force us. We must realize that life with God is by imitation, not by force. We are not to go to fatalism–everything that happens is God's will. Neither are we to operate on our own, independent of God–even thinking our role is to just do our best. Rather, we have to choose to abide, particularly knowing that apart from Him we can do nothing–zero, nil, zip.

- **Answered Prayer:** Christ states very clearly that IF we abide in Him (walking in His kingdom, in the Spirit, in Him through an intimate and ongoing relationship) and if His words abide in us, we can ask whatever we wish and it shall be done. Since we are understanding about surrender and the importance of following God's will, this does not mean that we, on our own, can decide what we want God to do. Rather, through our abiding we will understand His will and then can ask Him with confidence to fulfill that will. The "Word" here is "Rhema"–His application of the Written Word (Logos) to us personally; as we hear from Him (His Rhema Words to us from the

Scripture), we can expect that, as we fully understand the application of these promises to our personal lives, we will see it happen in reality.

We are to pray these with great boldness and confidence, knowing that the Father will change and bring about circumstances to fulfill what He has promised us. This is how He is glorified–that our circumstances change because we are experiencing God at work–His will in our lives. As we experience the supernatural changes, we will testify and bear witness that it was not us, but God. We are beginning to see that His will is not so much about what we are to do for Him, but rather what He wishes to do in and through us–impacting our circumstances that can reflect to the world His nature and His glory–and it requires abiding.

Our abiding is not Bible study, but rather a beautiful process of seeking His will; what He has to say and promise. Our role is to hear, process through to understanding, receive as true as it's now spoken to us, believed and then prayed in expectation that it will happen.

John 12:42-50:

42 Nevertheless even among the rulers many believed in Him, but because of the Pharisees they did not confess Him, lest they should be put out of the synagogue; 43 for they loved the praise of men more than the praise of God. 44 Then Jesus cried out and said, "He who believes in Me, believes not in Me but in Him who sent Me. 45 And he who sees Me sees Him who sent Me. 46 I have come as a light into the world, that whoever believes in Me should not abide in darkness. 47 And if anyone hears My words and does not believe, I do not judge him; for I did not come to judge the world but to save the world. 48 He who rejects Me, and does not receive My words, has that which judges him—the word that I have spoken will judge him in the last day. 49 For I have not spoken on My own authority; but the Father who sent Me gave Me a command, what I should say and what I should speak. 50 And I know that His command is everlasting life. Therefore, whatever I speak, just as the Father has told Me, so I speak."

As Jesus stated: If we abide in His word, we will know the truth and the truth will set us free. In John 12, He goes on to state an important aspect of His word–which is truth. It stands on its own and is not variable. He says that He has not come to judge the world, but that His word will judge. His will is rooted in truth. He wants us to realize that He does not violate this truth but that the Word stands as truth.

Thus, we have to be careful not to develop a theology where His forgiveness and love trumps truth. It does not. As a matter of fact, His love is so deep and profound that He does not alter His truth, which is why He invites us to abide in His truth. In Hebrews chapter 4, His word is described as a double-edged sword–that it cuts both ways, corresponding to Deuteronomy 30, where we learned that we must choose life and blessing versus death and cursing. Why? Because His word is truth and it stands on its own. If we choose to follow His word (His will), we will experience a blessing.

If we choose to reject or ignore His word, then we will experience death and cursing. And none of us are exempt. There's a tendency in the Christian community to think that all of our good works build up a reserve where we can be exempted from the consequences of poor choices. This is why Christ said we must daily deny self, take up our cross and follow Him, and that truth will be our judge. The good news (the Gospel) is that we don't have to be perfect. Rather, we need only have a heart to follow.

When we recognize we are operating in the flesh (self), there is an immediate remedy–repentance and returning back into the abiding relationship in Christ as He moves us forward into His beautiful will. The further good news is that no matter how long we have operated in the flesh and walked a long way from His will, He can restore it completely–now. We have a good picture of this in our modern technology called GPS.

As we get off track, the GPS voice in our car tells us to make a legal U-turn. This would be equivalent to repentance–turn around and get back on track. If we refuse because we think we know better, we just get further off track. Eventually, we come to a spot where it doesn't make any sense to return back to the original place, but rather the GPS says, "recalculating," and calculates out a brand new route to get us to our destination.

This is a great picture of how God works with us. He does not want us to live out a second, third, 100th or 1,000th best life, but rather upon our surrender and desire to walk into His will; we can experience His best because He can make His best work, no matter what or how far astray we might have gone. And it all starts with the fact that His truth stands on its own and is neither partial nor happenstance. We all are subject to this truth, and His desire is for us to live out His truth, which will lead us to His best and none better.

John 3:21-22:

"21 But he who does the truth comes to the light, that his deeds may be clearly seen, that they have been done in God." 22 After these things Jesus and His disciples came into the land of Judea, and there He remained with them and baptized.

We're all familiar with John 3:16—that the Father gave His only begotten Son that whoever believes in Him shall not perish. Many do not continue to read on to verse 22. There, He reiterates that His truth stands on its own. He says those that practice evil (operate in the self in their own will) stay away from the light that is His pure truth. Though they think they are living their own life to their best ability, they actually are experiencing the consequences of death and cursing, as well as often having God's hand against them. Rather, He desires that we would come to the light and experience the fullness of His will.

What this all means is that our abiding is a commitment to the light—to the truth. We should never be afraid of truth and always desire to hear, receive, understand and then follow the truth. It will lead us to the fullness of His will, which is best, and none better. This is where the process of discerning God's will is really rather simple. Our life is carried out day-by-day, step-by-step, decision-by-decision and is centered in the reality of our circumstances and the things we are facing.

65

We often approach God in a very binary way–should I do this or not? We have already decided what we would like to have happen and are seeking confirmation for our preference.

We actually are called to approach it quite differently. Instead of presuming the answer, we are to seek truth from God as a step-by-step process. That truth will reveal God's will as we receive that truth and understand that the truth stands on its own. For example, Linda and I were looking to do a 1031 exchange of one rental property to another. We had sold a property and were seeking alternatives as a next step. We discovered a particularly beautiful home that had been in foreclosure for three years and had sat empty during that whole time.

It was in a rather sad state of decay (entropy). On the lower level, we observed a large crack in the concrete foundation. Though it was beautiful with lots of upsides based on its low price, we needed to understand the truth about that foundation before we proceeded. If it was cosmetic, we would be confident to proceed, but if it were structural and required several hundred thousand dollars to fix and all the energy along with it, then our decision would be a no.

What we required was truth. So we hired a structural engineer (a trusted expert) that could give us an impartial evaluation of the situation. He had no vested interest in the outcome, but rather was paid to simply tell us the truth. Since we were neutral in seeking God's will, we were fully enthusiastic to receive his answer. If it was structural, then we would stop the process and keep looking; if it was cosmetic, we would proceed. That's why it is so simple. Seek truth, seek truth, seek truth. It takes all the pressure off of us and puts it squarely on God to reveal the truth and show us the way–knowing that He will never bait and switch us or have us receive something that we believe is true but is really false. We did buy the house, which turned into a true blessing. Our son, his wife and children moved into it–most enjoyable for them. We all had great memories there.

We have great confidence in His light because of His promises, as follows:

Psalm 25:1-5: Guides us into truth

1 A Psalm of David. To You, O Lord, I lift up my soul. 2 O my God, I trust in You; Let me not be ashamed; Let not my enemies triumph over me. 3 Indeed, let no one who waits on You be ashamed; Let those be ashamed who deal treacherously without cause. 4 Show me Your ways, O Lord; Teach me Your paths. 5 Lead me in Your truth and teach me, For You are the God of my salvation; On You I wait all the day.

As we have a heart to go to the light and embrace Him showing us His way and His paths, He promises to lead us in His truth. He does not leave it up to our own devices, but rather, since we seek truth willingly, He will make sure that we receive it. He is the one leading, not us. We can expect that and we are to process it so that we fully receive and understand it as we are seeking His step-by-step will. This includes all truth–truth about all the dynamics involved, the circumstances, the facts, the response of others involved, etc. As we are processing decisions and wanting to understand God's will, we are to keep "journaling" what we know, what we need to know, and what new truth God is revealing. He promises to guide us and lead us into truth.

Ephesians 5:8-14: As we walk in the light, we will know truth–the work of the Spirit.

8 For you were once darkness, but now you are light in the Lord. Walk as children of light 9 (for the fruit of the Spirit is in all goodness, righteousness, and truth), 10 finding out what is acceptable to the Lord. 11 And have no fellowship with the unfruitful works of darkness, but rather expose them. 12 For it is shameful even to speak of those things which are done by them in secret. 13 But all things that are exposed are made manifest by the light, for whatever makes manifest is light. 14 Therefore He says: "Awake, you who sleep, Arise from the dead, And Christ will give you light."

In Ephesians 5, Paul sets out keys to understanding God's will. He says to walk in love. (Remember that we have the privilege of walking with the Father because of the work of the Son, and it is not dependent on any prior work or spirituality on our part–it always begins and ends at the cross, and thus we are all equal at the cross.) Then, as we walk in that privilege, we are to walk in the light and walk in wisdom–seeking to understand what is acceptable to God and what is His will. As we walk–live it out moment by moment, day-by-day, step-by-step, and not once in a while or only for the big stuff, or only when we desire to be spiritual.

We will be led by the Holy Spirit into peace (Shalom–God's exceptional favor in our life) and righteousness–being transformed by God's righteous work in us and truth. We will receive clarity of all that is necessary to receive needed information, insight and discernment. He guarantees us that we will understand what is acceptable to Him and what exactly is His will. He promises that any truth necessary for us to receive this understanding will be given. Our commitment is to pursue it, and His commitment is to provide it. We can count on it.

David expresses our commitment in Psalm 51:6–that we are to have a strong desire (be delighted, take pleasure, be pleased) in seeking truth–in our inner soul (our heart). This cannot be just a mechanical thought. We are called to settle in our hearts that we truly want to know all truth (why would we not?). The truth leads us to His will which is best and none better. Thus, we should never suppress the truth, overlook the truth, deny the truth or rationalize the truth away. We are to have, from the center of our soul, a desire for truth; and He promises to reveal to us things that are hidden to give us great wisdom and prudence for walking forward into His will.

At another retreat, there was a couple who was admitted to struggling before they even arrived. The wife had desired to grow in Christ, but the husband was resistant and felt that most Christians were hypocrites, and thus not worth learning from. She and her friends convinced him to attend the retreat. We could tell that he was resistant and was rather non-participative, but did work through the Scriptures and the exercises of the retreat.

At the end of the retreat, we gathered together and asked each couple to share what they heard from God through the weekend. The husband started his sharing by stating that he had planned his escape from the retreat–that he was planning on leaving after the first night and having his wife's friends bring her back. He then shared that he was captivated by this concept of intimate abiding in the Vine and hearing from God–and that he had heard from God.

He openly confessed to his wife his resistance to God and asked for forgiveness. He committed to continue to grow together in Christ and to surrender their will to God's. This couple now is having the time of their life and they are both enjoying the fullness of transformed hearts and the fruit of the Spirit in their marriage, in their family and in their business. They realize that God's will is as much about transformation is it is about us fulfilling His assignments. They truly get it and are being transformed.

9

GOD'S WILL IS AS MUCH ABOUT WHO WE ARE BECOMING AS WHAT WE ARE DOING

Our focus tends to be on what are we supposed to do as we seek to follow God's will. However, we need to understand that how we are being called into the "doing" part of God's will is dependent upon the depth of our "becoming" part. His invitation to join His work never trumps His development and transformation of our character. The Father cares as much or more about our being transformed into the very nature of Christ as He cares about what we do. We, too, should equally care, and thus have a heart to cooperate with His transformation.

Romans 8:26-29: Spirit transforms us.

26 Likewise the Spirit also helps in our weaknesses. For we do not know what we should pray for as we ought, but the Spirit Himself makes intercession for us with groanings which cannot be uttered. 27 Now He who searches the hearts knows what the mind of the Spirit is, because He makes intercession for the saints according to the will of God. 28 And we know that all things work together for good to those who love God, to those who are the called according to His purpose. 29 For whom He foreknew, He also predestined to be conformed to the image of His Son, that He might be the firstborn among many brethren.

Romans (above) states that the Holy Spirit intercedes for us, according to the will of God. Thus, it is His role to continually receive instruction from the Father regarding His will and then communicate that to us. We have to be in the right spot at the right time to experience the fullness of His will. These verses then go on to tell us two important elements of His interceding work.

1. All things will work together for good. We can fully expect that God's sovereignty can make anything and everything work together for good. This includes our lousy choices of having not walked in the Spirit and experience the consequences of that. We tend to make a mess of things and experience the results of that mess. We often think that it is hopeless, and thus we are limited to a life of mediocrity.

   God states that His sovereignty is so powerful that He can restore us and return us to the full good because He can make everything work for our good. He defines this as useful, pleasant, agreeable, joyful, happy, excellent, distinguished and honorable. His good is spectacular, and we can believe that the Holy Spirit is at work, always inviting us to walk with Him so that He can make all things work together for good.

2. The purpose of His will is to have us conformed to the image of His Son. We are not to live a life of constant failure due to our sinful, selfish nature–rather, He has already determined to work all these things out so that we are not acting like Christ, but actually have been transformed to where Christ lives in us. It is His work. We can't transform ourselves, and we are called to believe that we will be transformed, as opposed to left alone fighting an unwinnable battle of the self. This is why Paul states in Galatians 2:20 that, "I have been crucified with Christ; it is no longer I who live, but Christ lives in me; and the life which I now live in the flesh I live by faith in the Son of God, who loved me and gave Himself for me. I do not set aside the grace of God; for if righteousness comes to the law, then Christ died in vain."

Our transformation is that the very nature of Christ will take over more and more of our soul so that it is Him living through us–His very nature is operating in and through us. It does not mean that we lose the essence of our soul–our will, our emotion, our personality, etc., but rather it is fulfilled as the very nature of Christ fills us and lives it out. Thus, it is our joy to be transformed and to experience the heart of God in us so that our perspective on life becomes His, and then we are fully able to enter into His will. This is described further as follows:

2 Corinthians 3:16-18: His metamorphosis means a changed nature.

16 Nevertheless when one turns to the Lord, the veil is taken away. 17 Now the Lord is the Spirit; and where the Spirit of the Lord is, there is liberty. 18 But we all, with unveiled face, beholding as in a mirror the glory of the Lord, are being transformed into the same image from glory to glory, just as by the Spirit of the Lord.

It is primary that Christ's objective for us, as we abide in Him, is to be transformed–truly changed in our nature. The key to this verse is "being transformed–metamorphosis"–caterpillar to butterfly. Can a butterfly go back to being a caterpillar? No, why not? Because its nature has been metamorphosed into a new nature. It cannot go back. That is what Christ offers and will do for us. Truly change us into His nature, one that does not manage our sinful nature and try to get better through performance, but rather through real change as we hear, receive and believe more of HIM, HIS Ways, His promises to us.

It will look like a heart that truly forgives, truly has compassion, truly able to speak the truth in love, etc.–not act like it, but truly have that be our nature. This happens, not all at once, but step-by-step (from glory to glory). He wants us to enjoy first grade, then go to second grade, etc. We never get to the end of it, but experience more of it as we age.

The promise is that where the Spirit is operating in our life we will experience liberty–freedom. Our life will not be burdened, full of fear, anxiety, anger, etc., but rather enjoying moment by moment our walk in the Spirit as He gives us this day our daily bread. It occurs now–where the Spirit of the Lord is ruling and leading in our lives. We need to understand that this does not happen after we are fully transformed, but rather during our daily journey of being transformed. We do not have to reach perfection in order to experience a liberty of the Spirit; we just have to be engaged in the very process itself. We will be being transformed all our life, step-by-step; so it happens during the journey.

We are able to have freedom now–not when something has been fulfilled, but now, as we daily walk with Him. This is important because we do not have to think there is a specific objective or maturity point that must be reached to have this freedom–it's now. We can remain in that interesting place of freedom now, and also in the "not yet" of being fully transformed. A beautiful truth that encourages us to walk and realize that the quality of the walk is to be free. If we are not experiencing this, it means we are back in the flesh and not abiding. Freedom is thus a good indicator for us to realize that we either are walking in the Spirit or need to return to the abiding relationship, and then continue on the journey with freedom.

Galatians 5:22-26: Fruit of Spirit is character.

22 But the fruit of the Spirit is love, joy, peace, longsuffering, kindness, goodness, faithfulness, 23 gentleness, self-control. Against such there is no law. 24 And those who are Christ's have crucified the flesh with its passions and desires. 25 If we live in the Spirit, let us also walk in the Spirit. 26 Let us not become conceited, provoking one another, envying one another.

We need to understand that this list is not fruits, but fruit. It is singular. It describes the whole fruit and is not to exclude any of its characteristics, but rather to include all of them as part of the whole. Furthermore, fruit is a product of the Spirit and not anything that we achieve on our own. We cannot fulfill our own character transformation–it is strictly a work of the Spirit. We need to further understand the true meaning of these characteristics, as opposed to trying to establish our own definition. These meanings are as follows:

Love: brotherly love, affection, good will, benevolence; joy: gladness, the cause or occasion of joy; peace: peace between individuals, i.e. harmony, concord, security, safety, prosperity, felicity, (because peace and harmony make and keep things safe and prosperous); patience: endurance, constancy, steadfastness, perseverance; kindness: goodness, integrity; goodness: upright heart and life; gentleness, humility; self-control (the virtue of one who masters his desires and passions, especially his sensual appetites).

Our character will be transformed into the nature of Christ as we abide. We are not to decide to obtain these qualities on our own–the more we try, the more we will fail, and thus get more discouraged and actually become less so. We, our spouses and our family, will be able to testify if these are becoming stronger in our life or not. There is no standard, arbitrary definition of these to judge each other by. We will simply be growing in this fruit of the Spirit month after month. The changes will be obvious and a key indicator that we are abiding. We should care as much about this as we care about what we are to do.

We need to receive how important this is to the Father as we live out our life as His children. He is living out His life through us. We, as children, sheep and branches, are to have the same quality of character as He has–His nature in us, so that the fruit is attractive to the world. Our life responses are actually His responses, out of our soul and who we are becoming, not what we are pretending to be or acting how we should be–but what we are from our souls. Our heart is then in sync with His, and the joy comes easily.

Remember, this is not something that we can decide to fulfill on our own (for example deciding we are going to become more patient), but rather it is a work of the Spirit. As we walk in the Spirit and abide in the Vine, we will experience this transformation. We will become more loving, more joyful, more patient, etc. We also must understand that there is no standard for this. My wife Linda is naturally more patient than me. My standard is not Linda, but rather that am I more patient than I was three months ago. It is simple to evaluate–ask our spouse, our good friend or our children.

They can verify that they are seeing a transformation, or challenge us that they have seen no transformation and, in fact, may have seen less of these qualities than previously. If they see no change, it simply means that we are not walking in the Spirit and abiding. If we are, we will experience the fruit of the Spirit. We are to relax, enjoy the abiding, and expect the transformation by the Spirit to be true transformation.

Isaiah 45:9-13: Clay, always being formed.

9 "Woe to him who strives with his Maker! Let the potsherd strive with the potsherds of the earth! Shall the clay say to him who forms it, 'What are you making?' Or shall your handiwork say, 'He has no hands?' 10 Woe to him who says to his father, 'What are you begetting?' Or to the woman, 'What have you brought forth?' " 11 Thus says the Lord, The Holy One of Israel, and his Maker: "Ask Me of things to come concerning My sons; And concerning the work of My hands, you command Me. 12 I have made the earth, And created man on it. I—My hands—stretched out the heavens, And all their host I have commanded. 13 I have raised him up in righteousness, And I will direct all his ways; He shall build My city And let My exiles go free, Not for price nor reward," Says the Lord of hosts.

Our hearts should always be ready for the Father to fully carry out His will in our lives, especially those elements that impact our character transformation. In these verses, Isaiah clearly sets forth that we are not to strive with our Maker, nor to question Him regarding what He is making, nor how He is impacting our lives. Rather, we are to be the clay to the potter. He is in charge, and He knows what is best. If we surrender as clay and allow Him to mold and shape us, we will be created into the nature of Christ and will experience the fullness of God's goodwill for us. We must remember that we are not to look at what is happening today as the end result, but that He has a larger story within a larger timeframe to create and mold us. Our hearts should always be on today.

Our prayer should be, "May Your will be done and may I fully cooperate with what You are doing." It is critical that, in order to experience what He is doing, we must live surrendered to Him, letting Him rule, walking in the Spirit and abiding in the Vine. Absent of that, we will not be His clay, but rather our own, and it will be messy. Adopt the perspective that He is not done yet, and that He is making something beautiful. Believe it, surrender to it and enjoy it.

Examples: Daniel 1:5-21; 3:8-30; 6:1-28:

5 And the king appointed for them a daily provision of the king's delicacies and of the wine which he drank, and three years of training for them, so that at the end of that time they might serve before the king. 6 Now from among those of the sons of Judah were Daniel, Hananiah, Mishael, and Azariah. 7 To them the chief of the eunuchs gave names: he gave Daniel the name Belteshazzar; to Hananiah, Shadrach; to Mishael, Meshach; and to Azariah, Abed-Nego. 8 But Daniel purposed in his heart that he would not defile himself with the portion of the king's delicacies, nor with the wine which he drank; therefore he requested of the chief of the eunuchs that he might not defile himself. 9 Now God had brought Daniel into the favor and goodwill of the chief of the eunuchs. 10 And the chief of the eunuchs said to Daniel, "I fear my lord the king, who has appointed your food and drink. For why should he see your faces looking worse than the young men who are your age? Then you would endanger my head before the king." 11 So Daniel said to the steward whom the chief of the eunuchs had set over Daniel, Hananiah, Mishael, and Azariah, 12 "Please test your servants for ten days, and let them give us vegetables to eat and water to drink. 13 Then let our appearance be examined before you, and the appearance of the young men who eat the portion of the king's delicacies; and as you see fit, so deal with your servants." 14 So he consented with them in this matter, and tested them ten days. 15 And at the end of ten days their features appeared better and fatter in flesh than all the young men who ate the portion of the king's delicacies. 16 Thus the steward took away their portion of delicacies and the wine that they were to drink, and gave them vegetables. 17 As for these four young men, God gave them knowledge and skill in all literature and wisdom; and Daniel had understanding in all visions and dreams. 18 Now at the end of the days, when the king had said that they should be brought in, the chief of the eunuchs brought them in before Nebuchadnezzar. 19 Then the king interviewed them, and among them all none was found like Daniel, Hananiah, Mishael, and Azariah; therefore they served before the king. 20 And in all matters of wisdom and understanding about which the king examined them, he found them ten times better than all the magicians and astrologers who were in all his realm. 21 Thus Daniel continued until the first year of King Cyrus.

In all these examples of Daniel's and his cohort's faith, they were already certain of God's truth and His will for them. When asked to eat food offered to idols, they had no difficulty saying no. However, instead of just taking a stand (based upon this truth), they asked God for wisdom and how to maneuver this scenario. God revealed that they were to ask for a test. They received favor in being given the opportunity for the test; and then God delivered on the results of the test so that they were given a "pass" on having to follow the king's order, and actually promoted per the king's order. God's will is not just following the truth as already known, but the individual steps in following this truth–unique and personal to the situation.

8 At this time some astrologers came forward and denounced the Jews. 9 They said to King Nebuchadnezzar, "May the king live forever! 10 Your Majesty has issued a decree that everyone who hears the sound of the horn, flute, zither, lyre, harp, pipe and all kinds of music must fall down and worship the image of gold, 11 and that whoever does not fall down and worship will be thrown into a blazing furnace. 12 But there are some Jews whom you have set over the affairs of the province of Babylon—Shadrach, Meshach and Abednego—who pay no attention to you, Your Majesty. They neither serve your gods nor worship the image of gold you have set up." 13 Furious with rage, Nebuchadnezzar summoned

Shadrach, Meshach and Abednego. So these men were brought before the king, 14 and Nebuchadnezzar said to them, "Is it true, Shadrach, Meshach and Abednego, that you do not serve my gods or worship the image of gold I have set up? 15 Now when you hear the sound of the horn, flute, zither, lyre, harp, pipe and all kinds of music, if you are ready to fall down and worship the image I made, very good. But if you do not worship it, you will be thrown immediately into a blazing furnace. Then what god will be able to rescue you from my hand?" 16 Shadrach, Meshach and Abednego replied to him, "King Nebuchadnezzar, we do not need to defend ourselves before you in this matter. 17 If we are thrown into the blazing furnace, the God we serve is able to deliver us from it, and he will deliver us from Your Majesty's hand. 18 But even if he does not, we want you to know, Your Majesty, that we will not serve your gods or worship the image of gold you have set up." 19 Then Nebuchadnezzar was furious with Shadrach, Meshach and Abednego, and his attitude toward them changed. He ordered the furnace heated seven times hotter than usual 20 and commanded some of the strongest soldiers in his army to tie up Shadrach, Meshach and Abednego and throw them into the blazing furnace. 21 So these men, wearing their robes, trousers, turbans and other clothes, were bound and thrown into the blazing furnace. 22 The king's command was so urgent and the furnace so hot that the flames of the fire killed the soldiers who took up Shadrach, Meshach and Abednego, 23 and these three men, firmly tied, fell into the blazing furnace. 24 Then King Nebuchadnezzar leaped to his feet in amazement and asked his advisers, "Weren't there three men that we tied up and threw into the fire?" They replied, "Certainly, Your Majesty." 25 He said, "Look! I see four men walking around in the fire, unbound and unharmed, and the fourth looks like a son of the gods." 26 Nebuchadnezzar then approached the opening of the blazing furnace and shouted, "Shadrach, Meshach and Abednego, servants of the Most High God, come out! Come here!" So Shadrach, Meshach and Abednego came out of the fire, 27 and the satraps, prefects, governors and royal advisers crowded around them. They saw that the fire had not harmed their bodies, nor was a hair of their heads singed; their robes were not scorched, and there was no smell of fire on them. 28 Then Nebuchadnezzar said, "Praise be to the God of Shadrach, Meshach and Abednego, who has sent his angel *and rescued his servants! They trusted in him and defied the king's command and were willing to give up their lives rather than serve or worship any god except their own God. 29 Therefore I decree that the people of any nation or language who say anything against the God of Shadrach, Meshach and Abednego be cut into pieces and their houses be turned into piles of rubble, for no other god can save in this way." 30 Then the king promoted Shadrach, Meshach and Abednego in the province of Babylon.*

In this situation, Daniel's cohorts were faced with death. They did not compromise on their beliefs and were willing to experience the full consequences of this choice. They knew God's will and were obedient to that will–and that God had the power to deliver them from the consequences. They left the results up to God. In this scenario, they were fully blessed–not only by being rescued but also in experiencing Christ himself through their trial. God's will is always bigger than we can imagine.

1 It pleased Darius to appoint 120 satraps to rule throughout the kingdom, 2 with three administrators over them, one of whom was Daniel. The satraps were made accountable to them so that the king might not suffer loss. 3 Now Daniel so distinguished himself among the administrators and the satraps by his exceptional qualities that the king planned to set him over the whole kingdom. 4 At this, the administrators and the satraps tried to find grounds for charges against Daniel in his conduct of government affairs, but they were unable to do so. They could find no corruption in him, because he was trustworthy and neither corrupt nor negligent. 5 Finally these men said, "We will never find any basis for charges against this man Daniel unless it has something to do with the law of his God." 6 So these administrators and satraps went as a group to the king and said: "May King Darius live forever! 7 The royal administrators, prefects, satraps, advisers and governors have all agreed that the king should issue an edict and enforce the decree that anyone who prays to any god or human being during the next thirty days, except to you, Your Majesty, shall be thrown into the lions' den. 8 Now, Your Majesty, issue the decree and put it in writing so that it cannot be altered—in accordance with the law of the Medes and Persians, which cannot be repealed." 9 So King Darius put the decree in writing. 10 Now when Daniel learned that the decree had been published, he went home to his upstairs room where the windows opened toward Jerusalem. Three times a day he got down on his knees and prayed, giving thanks to his God, just as he had done before. 11 Then these men went as a group and found Daniel praying and asking God for help.

12 So they went to the king and spoke to him about his royal decree: "Did you not publish a decree that during the next thirty days anyone who prays to any god or human being except to you, Your Majesty, would be thrown into the lions' den?" The king answered, "The decree stands—in accordance with the law of the Medes and Persians, which cannot be repealed." 13 Then they said to the king, "Daniel, who is one of the exiles from Judah, pays no attention to you, Your Majesty, or to the decree you put in writing. He still prays three times a day." 14 When the king heard this, he was greatly distressed; he was determined to rescue Daniel and made every effort until sundown to save him. 15 Then the men went as a group to King Darius and said to him, "Remember, Your Majesty, that according to the law of the Medes and Persians no decree or edict that the king issues can be changed." 16 So the king gave the order, and they brought Daniel and threw him into the lions' den. The king said to Daniel, "May your God, whom you serve continually, rescue you!" 17 A stone was brought and placed over the mouth of the den, and the king sealed it with his own signet ring and with the rings of his nobles, so that Daniel's situation might not be changed. 18 Then the king returned to his palace and spent the night without eating and without any entertainment being brought to him. And he could not sleep. 19 At the first light of dawn, the king got up and hurried to the lions' den. 20 When he came near the den, he called to Daniel in an anguished voice, "Daniel, servant of the living God, has your God, whom you serve continually, been able to rescue you from the lions?" 21 Daniel answered, "May the king live forever! 22 My God sent his angel, and he shut the mouths of the lions. They have not hurt me, because I was found innocent in his sight. Nor have I ever done any wrong before you, Your Majesty." 23 The king was overjoyed and gave orders to lift Daniel out of the den. And when Daniel was lifted from the den, no wound was found on him, because he had trusted in his God. 24 At the king's command, the men who had falsely accused Daniel were brought in and thrown into the lions' den, along with their wives and children. And before they reached the floor of the den, the lions overpowered them and crushed all their bones. 25 Then King Darius wrote to all the nations and peoples of every language in all the earth: "May you prosper greatly! 26 "I issue a decree that in every part of my kingdom people must fear and reverence the God of Daniel. "For he is the living God and he endures forever; his kingdom will not be destroyed, his dominion will never end. 27 He rescues and he saves; he performs signs and wonders in the heavens and on the earth. He has rescued Daniel from the power of the lions." 28 So Daniel prospered during the reign of Darius and the reign of Cyrus the Persian.

Here is another similar situation to Daniel's cohorts being thrown into the fire. Daniel was faced with hiding his prayer and worship to meet the king's new decree. He knew God's will—could not compromise and was willing to experience the consequences—death. He prayed for deliverance and God granted him favor—he was rescued; and the bigger story was that God was glorified. All were converted to worship the true God and Daniel prospered through the periods of the next two kings' reigns.

Daniel's stories are great examples of God's will—standing on the truth we already know without compromise; and then receiving discernment and clarity regarding the steps we are to take, leaving the results to God. We are to fully trust that God's will is best and none better, even if we are faced with dire consequences. We are to be part of His bigger story—a true privilege.

Linda and I have found that buying a one-year-old used car every 2 to 3 years is the most economical basis of owning a car. So we went to a dealer, found a one-year-old SUV and traded in our other car. Linda wanted to add some aftermarket features, such as DVD for the grandkids in the back, backup sensors and camera, etc. So the dealer kept the car for a few days to add all these aftermarket features. He called us two days later, and said that they found a crack in the radiator and were going to replace it at their expense. We thought, how good is that and said a delay was no problem.

However, when they did deliver the car a week later, Linda noticed that there were scratches on the car and some discoloration on the doors. She did not accept the car and sent it back. She said that she believed that something had happened to the car and that we should not accept it, and did not feel good about it in her spirit. The dealer called and said that it was just some overaggressive polishing and they would get it all taken care of. It must be noted here that I teach that one of the major principles of God's will is "coming to unity"—not just with each other, but also with God through the Spirit.

I told Linda that we already paid for the car, and it would be too difficult to unwind it all. The dealer promised to fix it all, so let's just accept the car. When they delivered it a second time, there still were some issues but, seemingly, not big enough to not accept it—though Linda disagreed and said we should not accept. Well, she was right. Within two weeks we experienced numerous issues, such as water coming through the back panel, wind whistling through the front windshield and the front panel falling off. Linda took it to another dealer for repair and he stated that something had happened to the car. It looked to him that it had fallen off of the lift when they were working on the aftermarket items, and that the entire car had been rebuilt.

He suggested we take it to a body shop to see all the things that had been replaced. We did, and we had two pages of items that what he had suspected was evidently true—that it had been completely rebuilt and all the parts, including the engine parts, were replaced. So, I called the dealer and let him know that obviously this car had been damaged and we wanted to return it and get another one. He apologized but wouldn't do it, and said to go ahead and sue him. The State of Colorado has a division for auto-dealer fraud, and so I filed a report, expecting the findings to prove our case since we had so much evidence. The department stated that they did know that the whole car had been damaged, but they could not prove it, as there was no evidence of any repairs in the system—so the dealer had committed fraud there as well.

I shared this with an attorney friend of mine, who joined me in my indignation and said that he would represent me for free to file a case against the dealer. So he sent me an outline to use to put facts together and build the case. He and I both felt that we needed to establish justice and that it was a righteous thing to do.

As I was filling out the forms, the Father said to me, "What are you doing?"

I said, "Setting things straight."

He said that I did not ask him, did not seek his will and was going down the wrong path. I said, "Whoops, I forgot about all that I know to be true." He said his will was for me not to pursue any lawsuit, to let it go, and to go get Linda new car (not even a one-year-old one, but brand new!). I said, "Yah, but if we keep her car one year I can financially make it all work." He said that this is one of the areas in which He wished to transform me, and to surrender to his will. I said, "Yah, but I'm going to lose a lot of money."

He said, "Yes, $8,000–write the check." So we traded her one-year-old car in for a brand-new car (and I disclosed everything about the car which, of course, meant a significantly lower value than blue-book), and I wrote an $8,000 check.

More importantly, at that juncture, the Father walked me through a transformation process of learning a deeper level of respecting Linda, walking in unity and dealing with my issue around finances. The Father cared more about who I was becoming and not the individual issues of the automobile. He used my disobedience and pride to bring me to a point of surrender and transformed heart. Even this was a joy.

10

HIS WILL IS SPECIFIC TO AND FOR US
EXPECT IT AND RELY UPON IT

1 John 5:14-15: He promises to speak it and make it known to us.

God states that if we ask anything according to His will, He hears us and it will be done. Thus, He must reveal His will to us so that we can pray it and experience the fulfillment of it in reality. Think about how simple yet critical this is. We are to pray according to His will. He must communicate His will to us personally so that we can pray it. He does not set up an impossible scenario where we are to pray according to His will, but He doesn't communicate that will–He doesn't say, "Good luck, I hope you guess it right but I'm not going to really tell you." If He sets up this requirement then He must fulfill His part of the requirement–He must communicate His will. Our role is to hear and continue to seek His will until it becomes clear to us.

We do not ask God to do something for us, but rather for us to receive and understand His will so that we can pray it and then expect the fulfillment of it. Often our prayers become our wish list of what we would like God to do in our particular situations. We are working to exercise our will and actually asking God to fulfill what we think is required or desired. God is asking us to join into His will–by receiving it with such clarity that we can pray it and then expect Him to fulfill it–which is His heart. He desires to reveal His supernatural power and His work in and through us. In all of our prayers, we are to begin with a critical first step–ask His will.

James 1:5-8: We are required to believe this.

5 If any of you lacks wisdom, let him ask (beg, call for, crave, desire, inquire of God(of God, who gives to all liberally (simply, openly, frankly, sincerely) and without reproach, and it will be given to him. 6 But let him ask in faith (conviction of the truth of anything, belief) with no doubting (to oppose, strive with dispute, contend), for he who doubts is like a wave of the sea driven and tossed by the wind. 7 For let not that man suppose that he will receive anything from the Lord; 8 he is a double-minded man, unstable in all his ways.

We all lack wisdom relating to all the things of life. We cannot pretend to know God's will by ourselves. Isaiah 55:8-9 tells us that His ways are not our ways and His thoughts are not our thoughts. His will is much more multi-dimensional and all-encompassing than we can ever imagine. Secondly, we lack wisdom on all of our decisions because we cannot see around the corner. Only God knows what lies ahead and how He desires for us to walk forward based upon the wisdom that He gives us. We tend to evaluate our decisions on the first 10 feet of 100-mile path. We evaluate pros and cons and determine which 10 feet looks best to us.

We can't possibly know what's down the road on this 100-mile path, especially around the corners that are invisible to us. However, God knows. He sees the whole hundred-mile path at once and knows which way to direct us. Recently, we took our grandchildren to a corn maze. They entered the maze and we went to the center and climbed up onto a tall platform. We could see the entire maze at once—they could only see their individual paths and walls. Often, they took wrong turns and wound up at dead-ends. Seeing the entire maze, we were able to instruct them by having them turn right, turn left or backup to find the right path that led them to freedom.

This is why we lack wisdom. What we see is limited, but He sees all. Our only requirement is to ask for this wisdom. There are no other conditions. Receiving wisdom is not dependent on our maturity, our skill, our holiness—rather, He promises to give us His wisdom (His will) generously and without finding fault: He will not require us to jump through hoops or fix anything because of our prior lack of seeking His will; He will just give it to us. The word "generously" also means with great clarity. It will not be fuzzy nor will it be confusing—it will be clear and we will understand it so that we can then move forward according to this wisdom. The wonderful thing is that the Father will communicate this wisdom (His will) in ways that we can understand–it is not dependent on a certain system or a certain level of maturity; it is His role to communicate it.

Currently, we have grandsons in sixth grade and fourth grade (Joshua and Aidan). Joshua is accelerating mentally so that he now has capability of understanding things far greater than Aidan (though, of course, both are brilliant. Opa–German for Grandpa–is obviously prejudiced). They can stand together and ask me the same question. I can communicate the answer so that Joshua understands completely. Aidan heard the same answer but will say he has no idea what I just said. I do not tell him that he should get with it; nor do I wait until he has become more mature. Rather, I alter my communication so that he can understand the answer. That is my role. This is exactly how God works. He has hundreds of ways to communicate wisdom and He will alter His message so that we can understand it based upon our ability to understand it. All we have to do is ask and He promises to answer. However, there is a condition–we must believe that He will give us the answer.

It is not required to, at first, believe what He says–that is a process; He moves us to faith (Hebrews 12:1-2 states that Christ is the author and finisher of faith, and Romans 10:17 says that faith comes from hearing and hearing from the Word). The magnificence of His will often astounds us and, upon our first hearing it, may appear too grand for us to believe. He fully understands that and just asks us to continue abiding until He finishes explaining it to the level of our faith so we can then believe it. All we have to understand is that, upon asking for wisdom, He will give it to us. If we do not believe this, He calls us double-minded (the word picture here is like a washing machine–back and forth, back and forth); and He will not be able to communicate His will. This actually is very practical.

If we ask for His will but do not believe that He will speak it, then if He did speak His will, we would still be wondering if it really was His will and become dependent on our own analysis. He says if that's where we stand then He will not bother communicating His will. So, we are called to get this very critical issue settled. We lack wisdom. We need His will. We are only to ask. He will give it to us. We are to believe that He will give it to us. If we have the issue settled, we begin to have wisdom and begin to understand His will with clarity. Ask, ask, ask.

Hebrews: 10:19-25, 35; Hebrews 11:3: Our special privilege.

19 Therefore, brethren, having boldness to enter the Holiest by the blood of Jesus, 20 by a new and living way which He consecrated for us, through the veil, that is, His flesh, 21 and having a High Priest over the house of God, 22 let us draw near with a true heart in full assurance of faith, having our hearts sprinkled from an evil conscience and our bodies washed with pure water. 23 Let us hold fast the confession of our hope without wavering, for He who promised is faithful. 24 And let us consider one another in order to stir up love and good works, 25 not forsaking the assembling of ourselves together, as is the manner of some, but exhorting one another, and so much the more as you see the Day approaching.

35 Therefore do not cast away your confidence, which has great reward. 36 For you have need of endurance, so that after you have done the will of God, you may receive the promise: 37 "For yet a little while, And He who is coming will come and will not tarry. 38 Now the just shall live by faith; But if anyone draws back, My soul has no pleasure in him."...11:1 Now faith is the substance of things hoped for, the evidence of things not seen. 2 For by it the elders obtained a good testimony. 3 By faith we understand that the worlds were framed by the word of God, so that the things which are seen were not made of things which are visible.

It is our special privilege to ask. The Father invites us directly into the throne room, where both the Son and the Spirit are already interceding on our behalf and receiving the Father's will for us. (Romans 8:26-34). We have this privilege because of the blood of Christ that was shed for us at the crucifixion. These verses use the truths about the holy of holies in the temple presented from the Old Testament.

The temple area was comprised of several sections. The first was the court of Gentiles, where non-Jews could come to worship Yahweh. The second court was the court of women, and the third court was the court of men. The inner court was the court for the Levites or priests to carry out their sacrifices. The holy of holies was reserved solely for the high priest once a year. The high priest would enter through the veil (an 80-foot high, eight inch thick curtain) on the Day of Atonement. Because he was the only one qualified to enter the holy of holies, they would tie a rope around his legs so that, if for some reason he died in the holy of holies, they could pull him back out since no one else could enter.

In the holy of holies, he would first sacrifice for himself, then another for his family and then a third one for the nation of Israel. Through the shedding of this blood he brought atonement (forgiveness) to himself, his family and then the nation of Israel. Since the offerings were not permanent and only valid for one year at a time, they had to be continually repeated by the high priest year after year.

When Christ died on the cross and shed His blood He was both the high priest and the sacrificial lamb. Through the shedding of His blood the veil was opened—at the time of His death on the cross, the veil was rent in two from top to bottom as a fulfillment of this truth. Instead of like before, when only the high priest could enter the holy of holies, now all believers can enter through the veil which has been opened and have communion directly with the Father, the Son and the Holy Spirit.

He tells us to enter this place of prayer with boldness—the word here means *freedom in speaking, unreservedness in speech, openly, frankly,* (i.e. without concealment, without ambiguity or circumlocution). He asks us to come with great confidence and boldness, marching right into the throne room and asking Him for wisdom. In fact, He tells us to come with a sincere or true heart—and the Greek word here means authentic—real, true, genuine, opposite to what is fictitious, counterfeit, imaginary, simulated or pretended; with this invitation of boldness and authenticity, He does not require us to establish our own level of holiness or establish our own ability to come to the throne room. That has already been given to us freely through the blood of Christ—and we all are equal at the foot of the cross. We have the same right to come to the throne room as the most eloquent and mature spiritual pastor that we might know.

We are just to come with an authentic heart. When we come, we are given the privilege of sharing our authentic hearts. We can talk to God and discuss anything including our frustrations, our anger, our disappointments and our difficulties; just open up completely and share our heart. Then we are to seek wisdom and hear His will—what is on His heart to communicate to us. He goes on to tell us to not throw away this great opportunity of coming to the throne with confidence. He actually says there will be reward—the word "reward" here means that we will be paid to come. (So worthwhile.) There is great benefit in coming to the throne room because we will be able to hear and understand His will—our great privilege as followers of Christ. He invites us to stay there until His will becomes clear to us and can turn into faith—which He defines as *certainty of things not seen*. The one thing that is not seen that we can be certain of is what someone speaks.

If I were to tell my wife that I would meet her at the Capital Grille restaurant in Denver at 6 p.m. on Friday night she would get in the car and go to the Capital Grille at 6 p.m. on Friday night. When I told her, it had not happened yet. But because I spoke it, she trusted me and she acted accordingly to her faith. She was certain that I would meet her there at that particular time on that particular day. What she didn't do was to talk herself out of it by saying that "he probably won't show up; doubt if he'll show up; probably he won't show up and therefore I guess it's not worth going." Nor did she call me every 30 minutes and ask, "Are you going, are you going, are you going?"

Rather, she had certainty of what I said and acted accordingly, and it happened just as I said. This is what the Father says is faith and, in fact, goes on to explain that the world was created by His spoken word; there was nothing until He spoke it into existence. What He says is so. His will as we receive it and believe it will be so. It will happen in reality. What a privilege we have to be able to march into the holy of holies and ask for God's will. Ask, ask, ask.

Is progressive, step-by-step:

Psalm 37:23: Steps ordered and established.
23 The steps of a good man are ordered by the Lord, And He delights in his way.

God delights (takes pleasure) in our way. Why? His will is done. The Lord has a specific path for us to walk down. We walk down that path step-by-step, and He orders or determines our steps. As we begin to understand His path, we realize that we are to receive and walk down the specific steps that He has already determined. He does not give us a broad path and say good luck–rather, He orders our steps.

Psalm 119:133: Steps directed.
133 Direct my steps by Your word, And let no iniquity have dominion over me.

He further tells us that our steps are directed and determined by His word, which is here called Rhema–what He personally speaks to us through His Spirit. The word "steps" here are footsteps and imply a step-by-step process. Again, He says He directs us and He gives step-by-step direction.

Proverbs 16:9: Steps directed.
9 A man's heart plans his way, But the Lord directs his steps.

God reminds us here that though we have a desire to plan our own way, He directs our steps. It means that He sets up, prepares and accomplishes our way step-by-step. All we can take is each step–one at a time. His will is revealed step-by-step–not all at once.

Deuteronomy 7:21-23: Little by little (we can't handle it all at once).

21 You shall not be terrified of them; for the Lord your God, the great and awesome God, is among you. 22 And the Lord your God will drive out those nations before you little by little; you will be unable to destroy them at once, lest the beasts of the field become too numerous for you. 23 But the Lord your God will deliver them over to you, and will inflict defeat upon them until they are destroyed.

As the Israelites crossed the Jordan and began to occupy the entire Promised Land, God told them that He would only give it to them little by little because they couldn't handle it all at once. The steps that we take are to be fully enjoyed, fully experienced, and are necessary for the next steps to come. Though we have a desire to know all the steps ahead of us for the next several months, God will only reveal them one by one. If we were to have all that information, we would either try to determine how to fulfill it on our own or become very passive and just wait until it happened–become fatalistic.

God only gives us the step-by-step instruction because He knows we can't possibly handle all of it at the same time. He desires to keep us dependent upon Him because He values our fellowship and uses the step-by-step approach to keep us abiding and intimate with Him. Step-by-step is absolutely the best possible way for us to live.

2 Corinthians 3:18: Glory to glory.

18 But we all, with unveiled face, beholding as in a mirror the glory of the Lord, are being transformed into the same image from glory to glory, just as by the Spirit of the Lord.

He tells us the same thing regarding our transformation. It is from glory to glory or step-by-step. He does not want us to fret that everything about us needs to be transformed immediately or we are falling short or disappointing Him. Rather that His work is to transform us (metamorphosis) one step at a time. Thus, we are called to enjoy each step and know that as we progress, we will continue to be transformed–step-by-step. Even when we are in our later years, we will still be transforming.

1 John 2:24-27: Progressive on what we know.

24 Therefore let that abide in you which you heard from the beginning. If what you heard from the beginning abides in you, you also will abide in the Son and in the Father. 25 And this is the promise that He has promised us—eternal life. 26 These things I have written to you concerning those who try to deceive you. 27 But the anointing which you have received from Him abides in you, and you do not need that anyone teach you; but as the same anointing teaches you concerning all things, and is true, and is not a lie, and just as it has taught you, you will abide in Him.

He tells us exactly how this works. As we abide and stand on the instruction and truth that we are receiving, we then receive the next step and further instruction. He says we don't have a need for other people to tell us God's will, but rather that we are all anointed by the Holy Spirit and will be instructed by the Holy Spirit. His will is progressive, so the next piece of His will relates to the step or the pieces that we already have received.

We are not to start over at every turn, but rather to continue down the path of the steps already taken. For example, a particular young CEO that I was discipling had left his previous job and was interviewing for his next job. He and his wife processed that an important step of God's will was that he would not travel more than two nights every other week because he had a marriage that needed further commitment and two young children at home that needed his energy.

Of course, after they had both received clarity about the step, he received a job offer at double the money he had ever made before, but travel four nights a week every week. It was tempting to go back to square one because of the money and to try to prove that this might be God's will. However, as we worked through this, he had to answer a simple question—what has God already said? He came to understand that he and his wife had already heard an important step and were to stand on that step.

Thus, he did not have to go through arduous prayer about this offer, but rather was already instructed by God to say no, which he did. A few weeks later, another offer came through equal to the money of the previous offer, but now only two nights every other week as God had clearly stated.

Remembering that His will is progressive, he was just given release to take the next step and determine if this company was truly worthy. He then had to move into due diligence to find out about their financial condition, the board makeup, the culture, the values, the freedom to hire, etc. All of the answers to these individual steps would determine God's will—as it is truly step-by-step.

As we progress step-by-step, we are to simply clarify what we know at the moment and not move past what we know. God's will is progressive and is based upon the truth that He gives us a step-by-step path. First, understand the step given and then continue to diligently seek the next step. It is progressive, and what we know now sets the stage for what we need to know next.

A senior executive friend of mine worked for a Fortune 500 company for over 30 years. He had career aspirations of potentially becoming the CEO and was certainly a viable candidate for this role. He had to learn to abide, to hear God's voice and surrender to God's will. As he was walking in the Spirit, he believed that the Father had spoken to him that it was time for him to retire. He began to dialogue with God, discuss what he was hearing with his wife and children, as well as friends such as myself.

Through this process of expecting to hear God's will, and knowing that it is step-by-step, he continued seeking wisdom and insight. One of the more important steps was for he and his wife and his daughter to define what it would look like if he were to retire—from all aspects: financial, use of time, ministry, board seats, consulting, marriage and family, etc. This took several months of processing as they began together to receive clarity about what this next phase would be. As he worked through all that he was receiving step-by-step, it became clear that God was calling him to retirement and that there was unity and confirmation from his wife, his daughter and his spiritual friends who could confirm in the Spirit's decision–this was God's will.

With this confidence and confirmation from God, he announced his retirement to the chairman in summer. He said that he would stay through December so that a replacement could be found, and he would be able to transition the work to the new person. It appeared that everything was in order and he was excited for this next phase. That next phase took quite a surprising turn–which I will share at the end of chapter 13.

11

PROCESS, PROCESS, PROCESS: ASK, SEEK, KNOCK

Luke 11:5-13:

5 And He said to them, "Which of you shall have a friend, and go to him at midnight and say to him, 'Friend, lend me three loaves; 6 for a friend of mine has come to me on his journey, and I have nothing to set before him'; 7 and he will answer from within and say, 'Do not trouble me; the door is now shut, and my children are with me in bed; I cannot rise and give to you'? 8 I say to you, though he will not rise and give to him because he is his friend, yet because of his persistence he will rise and give him as many as he needs. 9 "So I say to you, ask, and it will be given to you; seek, and you will find; knock, and it will be opened to you. 10 For everyone who asks receives, and he who seeks finds, and to him who knocks it will be opened. 11 If a son asks for bread a from any father among you, will he give him a stone? Or if he asks for a fish, will he give him a serpent instead of a fish? 12 Or if he asks for an egg, will he offer him a scorpion? 13 If you then, being evil, know how to give good gifts to your children, how much more will your heavenly Father give the Holy Spirit to those who ask Him!"

As we desire to receive His will step-by-step, the Lord lays out a very clear process of how to hear, understand and receive His will–persist in asking, seeking and knocking. As we have already seen in previous chapters, we are to actively ask for His will. Before we determine the steps in our own agenda, we are to back up a step and ask that His will be known to us. Remember, if we ask He promises to give it to us.

The story of the friend who knocked until the one who was in bed got up to give bread to Him was not about hammering God long enough until He finally gives us what we want–rather it was about persistence of seeking the answer to His will. He said he was not going to give him the answer because he was his friend (or believing child) but because he was persistent. Persistent in what? Persistent and staying with the process until he understood His will.

Had the one who was in bed said, "I will give you your needed food tomorrow morning," he would've gone home and come back the next day. He just needed to know the answer, as we do. With this persistence, God gives us a very clear process–ask, seek, knock. Ask for His will to be known and then fully believe that it will be given to us with great clarity. Then seek for it as if it were lost treasure. The word "seek" here means: *to find, to seek a thing, to seek [in order to find out] by thinking, meditating, reasoning, to enquire into, to seek after, seek for, aim at, strive after, to seek i.e. require, demand, to crave, demand something from someone.* We are to do our due diligence and continue to look for facts, information, truth, new understanding, as we attempt to move forward step-by-step. This is our activity as we understand that God will give us the truth during our due diligence.

If one of your relatives called you and said that they hid three gold bars in your house and if you could find them they would be yours, you would look for them in every place in the house until you found them. You know that they are there, just not specifically where, so you would seek them until you found them. This is a picture of what it means to seek–look everywhere in every place until you reach clarity of His will. Never be afraid of new information. As you understand needed information, go after it to the fullest you can. An example: As we seek and move to clarity of God's will, there will be specific opportunities to determine if this particular answer really is God's will.

We then move into the phase of knocking to see if God opens the door or closes it or leaves it closed and wants us to continue. Again, He will not bait or switch us. If we knock and it opens, go through the door. But realize that the door may just be opening to another path or another hallway and that the specific door you were hoping for may be down the road. It is just a process of having us narrow the options so that we move toward exactly what He desires. If the door is closed, we are not to knock it down ourselves. This is tricky since often we see an answer or alternative that looks attractive. We think this is the answer, and thus try hard to make it so.

We are to let the door open or close. One time Linda and I were working alternatives for our Europe retreat. One of our requirements was that the gathering room provided by the castle or hotel must be set up as a living room with couches and easy chairs. We had two great options, with one preferred because of the amenities. However, that one returned their contract stating that it could not guarantee the living room scenario, so we considered that door closed and went with the other option. It was a grand time, and we probably will never know the full extent of why this place was God's will and not the other–though we knew it clearly was.

We are always neutral to receive His answer, and He does it at that moment through open and closed doors. Our role is strictly to knock and then let Him either open or close the door. It is such a freeing and beautiful process because it is His work and not ours. We are just asked to seek and knock until we have clarity and confirmation that we are exactly in His will, which will be specifically geared to us.

He wants us to have confidence that He will show us the way step-by-step, and will not hide the truth or make us guess at the truth. He tells us that He actually gives us the Holy Spirit, who fully knows the answer. He will get us the answer all the time and every time. This is not difficult for Him since we have the Holy Spirit resident within us, and His job is to guide us into all truth.

We are to have persistence in seeking His will–stay with it until we find it; look for it as you would a lost treasure; do not give up, continue to seek and then let Him open and close doors as we move into specific answers. To put this process into practice on something very specific, follow these steps:

1. Write out what is the question at hand: the decision, problem, issue, what is on your heart.

2. Write out what we know: truth; certain; clear.

3. Write out what we do not know: fuzzy; uncertain; not clear; info needed.

4. Ask for His will, seek the answers to each step, and continue until opportunities to knock and then find fulfillment of His will.

   It is helpful to process these with your spouse or another fellow believer who can help clarify what is known, what needs to be known, and what steps to take next to seek answers. Let it be a true joy in the adventure of understanding His will–step-by-step.

Seek, receive, understand His Instructions:
In the seeking process, it is important to receive and understand His instruction:

Matthew 23:10: Remember, only He is our instructor!! (and no one else).
10 And do not be called teachers; for One is your Teacher, the Christ.

It is important that we are seeking His will and no one else's. We are not to gather everyone's opinion and guess or evaluate which is best, but rather to continue to seek His answers, especially since He promises to get us His answers. Don't be swayed by your own desires and thinking or by the advice of others. We will see that it is helpful to have others come alongside of you but not as your primary way of determining God's will. He is our instructor, and we can trust that He will fulfill and deliver His instruction to us.

Job 22:21-30: Abide, receive–in His kingdom, seek Him and put Him first.

21 "Now acquaint yourself with Him, and be at peace; Thereby good will come to you. 22 Receive, please, instruction from His mouth, And lay up His words in your heart. 23 If you return to the Almighty, you will be built up; You will remove iniquity far from your tents. 24 Then you will lay your gold in the dust, And the gold of Ophir among the stones of the brooks. 25 Yes, the Almighty will be your gold And your precious silver; 26 For then you will have your delight in the Almighty, And lift up your face to God. 27 You will make your prayer to Him, He will hear you, And you will pay your vows. 28 You will also declare a thing, And it will be established for you; So light will shine on your ways. 29 When they cast you down, and you say, 'Exaltation will come!' Then He will save the humble person. 30 He will even deliver one who is not innocent; Yes, he will be delivered by the purity of your hands."

As we abide in Him, we will be at peace and will receive His instruction. We receive His instruction by putting Him first above all else–particularly anything financial. This is one of the biggest issues of seeking His will–that we often think that financial gain is always God's answer–it is not. He cares more about our freedom and our joy in life than material wealth. It doesn't mean that He won't bless us with material wealth, but it is not the criteria to determine His will. He is. We are to pray, hear His will and then declare it clearly. This process of declaration is important as we move step-by-step.

We are to declare what we know, and if we are certain of His will to declare that as well. Declaring that gives us the confidence to know that we have clarity. If we cannot declare it, then we just need to understand that it is not yet clear to us, and we cannot boldly declare it. That is actually very good, as it causes us to continue to seek His answers step-by-step. If we can declare it, then we can begin to pray and expect it to happen in reality. God's will isn't hypothetical–it is real. As we understand it, we declare it and then we will be able to bear witness to the reality of it when it happens–a beautiful and exciting life of adventure.

Proverbs 2:1-13: Receive, receive–go after it.

1 My son, if you receive my words, And treasure my commands within you, 2 So that you incline your ear to wisdom, And apply your heart to understanding; 3 Yes, if you cry out for discernment, And lift up your voice for understanding, 4 If you seek her as silver, And search for her as for hidden treasures; 5 Then you will understand the fear of the Lord, And find the knowledge of God. 6 For the Lord gives wisdom; From His mouth come knowledge and understanding; 7 He stores up sound wisdom for the upright; He is a shield to those who walk uprightly; 8 He guards the paths of justice, And preserves the way of His saints. 9 Then you will understand righteousness and justice, Equity and every good path. 10 When wisdom enters your heart, And knowledge is pleasant to your soul, 11 Discretion will preserve you; Understanding will keep you, 12 To deliver you from the way of evil, From the man who speaks perverse things, 13 From those who leave the paths of uprightness To walk in the ways of darkness;

As stated previously, as we seek answers we are to be aggressive: go after it. The Scripture presents to us an, 'if–then' statement, which means it is conditional. If we walk with God according to the requirements set forth by aggressively pursuing wisdom, then we will receive the blessings promised–the wisdom and His will which fulfills His life for us. Let's review this process:

Requirements:

1. Receive His words

2. Treasure His instructions

3. Desire to process and received wisdom and understanding

4. Cry out for discernment

5. Seek God's wisdom as if it were hidden treasure

Promised blessings:

1. Understand and live in the fear of the Lord

2. Find out what it means to know and experience God

3. Receive wisdom, knowledge and understanding

4. Be protected and guarded

5. Understand righteousness, fairness

6. Understand every good path that we walk will lead to goodness

7. Wisdom will enter our souls and be pleasant

8. We will be delivered from the way of evil and from those who oppose us

Why would we not? Our role is to go after wisdom, and He promises to show us every path He has planned. It is specific to us and is precious for us. Even though we live in a troublesome world, and we will have adversity and obstacles, the path will be pleasant and we will see and experience God's beautiful plan for us.

Proverbs 4:1-12; 20-23: Pay attention.

1 Hear, my children, the instruction of a father, And give attention to know understanding; 2 For I give you good doctrine: Do not forsake my law. 3 When I was my father's son, Tender and the only one in the sight of my mother, 4 He also taught me, and said to me: "Let your heart retain my words; Keep my commands, and live. 5 Get wisdom! Get understanding! Do not forget, nor turn away from the words of my mouth. 6 Do not forsake her, and she will preserve you; Love her, and she will keep you. 7 Wisdom is the principal thing; Therefore get wisdom. And in all your getting, get understanding. 8 Exalt her, and she will promote you; She will bring you honor, when you embrace her. 9 She will place on your head an ornament of grace; A crown of glory she will deliver to you." 10 Hear, my son, and receive my sayings, And the years of your life will be many. 11 I have taught you in the way of wisdom; I have led you in right paths. 12 When you walk, your steps will not be hindered, And when you run, you will not stumble.

20 My son, give attention to my words; Incline your ear to my sayings. 21 Do not let them depart from your eyes; Keep them in the midst of your heart; 22 For they are life to those who find them, And health to all their flesh. 23 Keep your heart with all diligence, For out of it spring the issues of life.

As we are in the Word, He will reveal the key elements of His will through His word to us. The key is to pay attention to what the Lord is speaking to us–not just doing a devotion or our own idea of Bible study–rather to be listening and processing what He is speaking and has on His heart to reveal to us. This will be where we have high interest; where there is a word or idea shown to us over and over (we might hear it at church, see it on TV, in a book, etc.); and where we have a strong desire to pursue the issue further because it is stimulating our heart.

We are called to stay with it (pay attention) until the Words and the truth of the living Words get into the middle of our hearts (souls). We are to understand them, receive them, process them, and then believe them. When we arrive at belief (remember, it is a process of Christ perfecting faith in us), we then, with confidence, can pray the promise of these Words. We then are to have an expectation that they will be so (AMEN) in our real lives–both in circumstances and in the transformation of our hearts that lead us to freedom.

Matthew 25:21: Be faithful to what we know is true.

21 His lord said to him, 'Well done, good and faithful servant; you were faithful over a few things, I will make you ruler over many things. Enter into the joy of your lord.'

Being faithful to small things means that we are faithful to what we know to be true. As we are receiving instruction from His word and what He is speaking personally to us through our ask, seek and knock process, we are to trust these truths and stand on these truths. Do not violate these truths nor neglect these truths–rather be faithful to these truths. They will guide us to His true will step-by-step.

- ◆ Know that His will is primarily what He promises to do for, in, through us (and what He does is supernatural!)– this is the essence of His will–what He is doing.

As we pursue God's will, we usually pursue it relative to our perspective alone; what decisions are we to make, what are we to do, what are we to understand. Interestingly, His will is actually, most of all, what He wishes to do in our lives. Through our redemptive life, we are to glorify Him. We are to demonstrate and manifest to principalities and powers (Ephesians 3:13) the supernatural work of God. His will involves us being at the right place at the right time with the right people in order to experience His planned supernatural work. Thus, as we are seeking wisdom and understanding, He guides us step-by-step not just for our own personal benefit, but rather to join His bigger story and demonstrate His supernatural work in and through our circumstances. Please review the following:

2 Corinthians 1:18-24: ALL promises are true IN Christ Jesus.
18 But as God is faithful, our word to you was not Yes and No. 19 For the Son of God, Jesus Christ, who was preached among you by us—by me, Silvanus, and Timothy—was not Yes and No, but in Him was Yes. 20 For all the promises of God in Him are Yes, and in Him Amen, to the glory of God through us. 21 Now He who establishes us with you in Christ and has anointed us is God, 22 who also has sealed us and given us the Spirit in our hearts as a guarantee. 23 Moreover I call God as witness against my soul, that to spare you I came no more to Corinth. 24 Not that we have dominion over your faith, but are fellow workers for your joy; for by faith you stand.

We begin with an important truth about promises: All the promises of God are "yes" in Christ Jesus. There are two key principles supporting this simple statement:

1. God's promises are not yes and no but all are completely "yes." This means that they are not "perhaps" or "maybe." This is important, so that we realize that there aren't just a few lucky people to receive promises or that His promises are only available to us once in a while. They are always "yes" and available to all of us without partiality. Thus, if we receive a promise from God, we can have confidence that it is meant for us and is fully available to us.

2. The promises, that are always "yes," are available to us only as we are "in Christ." If we are not in Christ we are automatically disqualified from receiving the promises. Thus, though they are all "yes," they can only be realized as we walk in Christ. It is good to make a comment here that when we hear "maybe," we tend to believe "probably not." God wants us to recognize that He does not say "maybe" but "yes," and that this important principle is key to us understanding and desiring to experience the fullness of His promises to us.

Our response is to say "Amen," which means: *so it is, so be it, may it be fulfilled.* It was a custom, which passed over from the synagogues to the Christian assemblies, that when one had read, discoursed or had offered up solemn prayer to God, the others responded "Amen," and thus made the substance of what was uttered their own. As we speak "Amen" we say, "We understood Your will, received Your promise to us, and now, praying that it will happen in reality—so be it: Amen."

Further, that this is all for His glory, magnificence, excellence, pre-eminence, dignity, grace, majesty, a thing belonging to God, the kingly majesty which belongs to Him as supreme ruler, majesty in the sense of absolute perfection of the deity. His promises are His commitment to us–He desires to deliver amazing things to us through us hearing them, receiving them and then believing them. As they are delivered, we will bear witness and glorify Him. All of His promises are "yes."

Ephesians 3:15-21: Working in us, through us and around us (circumstances)–may be more exceptional than we could ever imagine or think.

15 from whom the whole family in heaven and earth is named, 16 that He would grant you, according to the riches of His glory, to be strengthened with might through His Spirit in the inner man, 17 that Christ may dwell in your hearts through faith; that you, being rooted and grounded in love, 18 may be able to comprehend with all the saints what is the width and length and depth and height—19 to know the love of Christ which passes knowledge; that you may be filled with all the fullness of God. 20 Now to Him who is able to do exceedingly abundantly above all that we ask or think, according to the power that works in us, 21 to Him be glory in the church by Christ Jesus to all generations, forever and ever. Amen.

As the Holy Spirit strengthens our inner man and moves us into His will to experience the fullness of Christ and the depth of His love, He tells us to ask specifically for God to do immeasurably more than we could ask or imagine. He lifts us from thinking about what we can achieve for Him or fulfill on our own power to what incredible things He would like to do in our real circumstances. He wants to demonstrate the exceedingly, abundantly to us (what is beyond, superior, extraordinary, surpassing, uncommon). It is to be truly spectacular.

He actually invites us to ask and think big and then pray that He will reveal His supernatural will which is far above what we can think or imagine. This stimulates us to begin being creative and expensive so that we are open to His grand purposes and His grand promises.

Hebrews 2:1-4: His will is for us to experience supernatural miracles, signs and wonders.

1 Therefore we must give the more earnest heed to the things we have heard, lest we drift away. 2 For if the word spoken through angels proved steadfast, and every transgression and disobedience received a just reward, 3 how shall we escape if we neglect so great a salvation, which at the first began to be spoken by the Lord, and was confirmed to us by those who heard Him, 4 God also bearing witness both with signs and wonders, with various miracles, and gifts of the Holy Spirit, according to His own will?

He encourages us not to neglect so great a salvation. We neglect by being careless and lazy and not really expecting God to act in a magnificent way. He states clearly that God will bear witness to our personal salvation with signs, wonders, miracles and gifts of the Holy Spirit. We will see the miraculous. It is supposed to be normal, as it was in the early church as they had God bear witness to their boldly speaking the truth of Christ with signs, wonders, miracles and supernatural power. It is not intended to be just for the few once in a while. His will is the supernatural. Neglect would mean that we would suppress this possibility and drift back to just the natural and what we can do ourselves. Look to and expect the supernatural.

Romans 12:3-8: Manifested as we are joining His will.

3 For I say, through the grace given to me, to everyone who is among you, not to think of himself more highly than he ought to think, but to think soberly, as God has dealt to each one a measure of faith. 4 For as we have many members in one body, but all the members do not have the same function, 5 so we, being many, are one body in Christ, and individually members of one another. 6 Having then gifts differing according to the grace that is given to us, let us use them: if prophecy, let us prophesy in proportion to our faith; 7 or ministry, let us use it in our ministering; he who teaches, in teaching; 8 he who exhorts, in exhortation; he who gives, with liberality; he who leads, with diligence; he who shows mercy, with cheerfulness.

These verses give further detail about the very gifts of the Holy Spirit. In the Christian church there is a misunderstanding about the gifts of the Holy Spirit. Many think that they ceased in the first century (which means that much of the New Testament is worthless to us now) or that only certain people have these special gifts. As members of the Body of Christ we are all to experience all of these gifts as determined by the Holy Spirit. It is not specific to our personal skills, but rather to the work of the Holy Spirit as we join Him in His will, day-by-day, step-by-step. Manifest these gifts as He so wills, according to His purposes and timing - and these gifts are supernatural, as follows:

♦ *Wisdom: the act of interpreting dreams and always giving the sagest advice, discovering the meaning of things not normally known, skill in the management of affairs and decisions.*

♦ *Knowledge: understanding, perception, insight.*

♦ *Faith: conviction of the truth of anything, belief in God and divine things, deep trust.*

♦ *Healing: to cure, heal, to make whole, to free from errors and sins, to bring about (one's) salvation.*

♦ *Miracles: strength, power, ability, for performing things not naturally occurring.*

♦ *Prophecy: a discourse emanating from divine inspiration and declaring the purposes of God, whether by reproving and admonishing the wicked, or comforting the afflicted, or revealing things hidden; especially by foretelling future events.*

♦ *Discernment: to separate, make a distinction, decide, to determine, give judgment, decide a dispute.*

♦ *Tongue: the language or dialect used by a particular people distinct from that of other nations.*

♦ *Interpretation: to translate what has been spoken or written in a foreign tongue into the vernacular.*

His miraculous gifts are intended for us to exercise them for the purposes of edifying the body and joining God's bigger story. We will be thrilled at personally experiencing these but are not to be seeking the gifts—just to enjoy being in God's will where these gifts will be experienced and given away. It will glorify Him as we assist each other in growing in these gifts.

Daniel 4:1-3; 6:25-28: Signs and wonders normal.

4:1 Nebuchadnezzar the king, To all peoples, nations, and languages that dwell in all the earth: Peace be multiplied to you. 2 I thought it good to declare the signs and wonders that the Most High God has worked for me. 3 How great are His signs, And how mighty His wonders! His kingdom is an everlasting kingdom, And His dominion is from generation to generation.

6:25 Then King Darius wrote: To all peoples, nations, and languages that dwell in all the earth: Peace be multiplied to you. 26 I make a decree that in every dominion of my kingdom men must tremble and fear before the God of Daniel. For He is the living God, And steadfast forever; His kingdom is the one which shall not be destroyed, And His dominion shall endure to the end. 27 He delivers and rescues, And He works signs and wonders In heaven and on earth, Who has delivered Daniel from the power of the lions. 28 So this Daniel prospered in the reign of Darius and in the reign of Cyrus the Persian.

As Daniel reflects on the nature of God, he sets forth that signs and wonders and miracles are normal. Why? It is God's nature to perform and demonstrate the miraculous—and they are great!! He is the one who works them!! Where? In our lives. It is His joy to work them. Expect it.

Acts 2:40-46; 4:23-31; 5:12-16: Miracles daily.

2:40 And with many other words he testified and exhorted them, saying, "Be saved from this perverse generation." 41 Then those who gladly received his word were baptized; and that day about three thousand souls were added to them. 42 And they continued steadfastly in the apostles' doctrine and fellowship, in the breaking of bread, and in prayers. 43 Then fear came upon every soul, and many wonders and signs were done through the apostles. 44 Now all who believed were together, and had all things in common, 45 and sold their possessions and goods, and divided them among all, as anyone had need. 46 So continuing daily with one accord in the temple, and breaking bread from house to house, they ate their food with gladness and simplicity of heart,

4:23 And being let go, they went to their own companions and reported all that the chief priests and elders had said to them. 24 So when they heard that, they raised their voice to God with one accord and said: "Lord, You are God, who made heaven and earth and the sea, and all that is in them, 25 who by the mouth of Your servant David have said: 'Why did the nations rage, And the people plot vain things? 26 The kings of the earth took their stand, And the rulers were gathered together Against the Lord and against His Christ.' 27 "For truly against Your holy Servant Jesus, whom You anointed, both Herod and Pontius Pilate, with the Gentiles and the people of Israel, were gathered together 28 to do whatever Your hand and Your purpose determined before to be done. 29 Now, Lord, look on their threats, and grant to Your servants that with all boldness they may speak Your word, 30 by stretching out Your hand to heal, and that signs and wonders may be done through the name of Your holy Servant Jesus." 31 And when they had prayed, the place where they were assembled together was shaken; and they were all filled with the Holy Spirit, and they spoke the word of God with boldness

5:12 And through the hands of the apostles many signs and wonders were done among the people. And they were all with one accord in Solomon's Porch. 13 Yet none of the rest dared join them, but the people esteemed them highly. 14 And believers were increasingly added to the Lord, multitudes of both men and women, 15 so that they brought the sick out into the streets and laid them on beds and couches, that at least the shadow of Peter passing by might fall on some of them. 16 Also a multitude gathered from the surrounding cities to Jerusalem, bringing sick people and those who were tormented by unclean spirits, and they were all healed.

The early church routinely experienced miracles as the people came together in small groups. These were in the form of signs and wonders, supernatural activity and amazing demonstrations of God's power in many, many situations. As people experienced these miracles, they had enthusiasm for glorifying Him, bearing witness to Him and inviting others to come and enjoy these miracles. God's will is just not about us doing the right thing—but doing His thing.

Being in the right place at the right time with the right people so that God can work His mighty power in our circumstances—and that is why our circumstances are not too difficult for Him. In fact, difficult circumstances that are normal are necessary for Him to demonstrate His power. If it were not needed then we would not pursue the miraculous, nor expect it. Miracles are to be a part of our everyday life because our life needs them—and God is more than pleased to deliver them—His will. If we were to live as the early church did, we would again see an explosion of people coming to Christ and living the life of the supernatural—and then more people coming to Christ.

John 14:10-18: His will for sure—join His mighty works.

10 Do you not believe that I am in the Father, and the Father in Me? The words that I speak to you I do not speak on My own authority; but the Father who dwells in Me does the works. 11 Believe Me that I am in the Father and the Father in Me, or else believe Me for the sake of the works themselves. 12 "Most assuredly, I say to you, he who believes in Me, the works that I do he will do also; and greater works than these he will do, because I go to My Father. 13 And whatever you ask in My name, that I will do, that the Father may be glorified in the Son. 14 If you ask anything in My name, I will do it. 15 "If you love Me, keep My commandments. 16 And I will pray the Father, and He will give you another Helper, that

110

He may abide with you forever— 17 the Spirit of truth, whom the world cannot receive, because it neither sees Him nor knows Him; but you know Him, for He dwells with you and will be in you. 18 I will not leave you orphans; I will come to you.

The works of God's miracles are intended to drive us to believe that He is the Almighty God, that He is all-powerful and that He deeply cares for us with a heart to deliver supernatural works in our lives. He tells us that we will experience these works as a normal way of life as we learn to ask for His will in His name—what He speaks under His authority and what He wishes to deliver. The works are not ours, nor do we have an automatic right to experience these works. Rather, we are to seek His will and, as part of His will, He promises that we will work these works. It is not limited nor is it periodic. We all are to experience the supernatural as we pray in His name.

The way that the Father led us into His will for our retreat ministry is quite an amazing example of these truths. Our son, Peter, and his wife, Shara, had moved to Germany after graduating from college where Peter helped set up a new operation with a client of mine. Peter speaks fluent German and Shara speaks fluent French so together they were having a grand time in Europe as they began their marriage. Linda and I wanted to visit them. (Over the years I have learned to create exceptional vacations together in spectacular places.)

So I found on the Internet a castle outside Vienna, Austria–25,000 square foot, 15 bedrooms, with a moat!! It was rather expensive, and too large for just our family, so I called some executive friends and asked them if they'd wish to join us in Europe and share the cost of the castle. Four couples were excited at the prospect and eventually met up with us in Austria. Our plan was to go sightseeing every day and join the castle chef for dinner every night in their over-the-top dining room.

The first day, I asked the group if we could do a devotion in the Word together, and everyone said, "Sure, would be good for us." Three and half hours later we were amazed at how powerful this time was in the Word. They all asked if we could do it the next day and, again, we spent three and a half hours in the Word, with a spiritual experience that was beyond anything we had had before. So they asked if we could just do it each day of the week. At the end of having done the seven days in a row, we had amazing revelation, insight into God's will for each of us, and transformation in our marriages.

The understanding that Linda and I, regarding abiding, went to a higher level as we moved from Bible study to abiding in the Vine through the Holy Spirit. We all had heard from God personally and directly, including all in our family. After we had returned back to the states, Linda and I realized how precious this experience was and heard the Father speak to us to plan to do it again the following year. The couples that had come the first year shared it with others and we actually had two groups the second year–in a beautiful castle in Scotland.

This time we formalized the structure by spending time in the Word each morning through lunch, doing sightseeing in the afternoon, where couples could go off on their own and process what they were hearing, and then come back to the castle for an exceptional dinner with the chef. Our dinners were truly European experiences–we sat around in sweet fellowship for three to four hours, enjoying the meal and open dialogue about what we were hearing from God and what it all meant to us as couples. Again, we experienced supernatural revelation, understanding of God's will and transformation intermarriages.

We knew then that God was calling us into something special, so we went through the "ask, seek and knock" process of formalizing this further. We asked the Father to reveal His will about this growing ministry and began seeking his steps. We had the participants from the first two groups tell us what was so special and what worked well and what didn't work well. We put together a list and prayed through how to formalize the process, which had to include plenty of room for the Holy Spirit to work while we were conducting the retreats. From the two prior groups they sent us names of people who had a potential interest, and we "knocked" on their doors to see if they opened. We had so many open that we had to have three groups the following year, which we met with at a castle in Loire Valley, France.

Again, we experienced supernatural revelation, understanding of God's will and transformation of our marriages. Upon returning, Linda and I received confirmation that this was now to become a priority for us, so we went further in the "ask, seek, and knock" process for what was next. We discovered that there were many people who would like to experience this type of retreat, but could not afford the cost or a full week in Europe. So we asked the Father if we should bring the ministry to the U.S. on weekends. He said, "YES, get going."

We then opened up our house for a retreat every other month in Castle Pines, Colorado and had no difficulty in filling up the weekends. We never advertised the ministry at all–it was all word-of-mouth and all were experiencing the beauty of hearing from God and having their marriages and lives transformed (we also did several singles retreats). Linda and I were thoroughly enjoying "giving it away" in this retreat ministry as we had discovered that it wasn't up to us to teach anything–rather, bringing people together to explore truth in the Word and they would begin hearing from God and learning what it means to abide in the Vine; and discovering the beauty of following God's will.

12

HIS WILL IS SECRET

HE REVEALS SECRET THINGS FROM HIS "SECRET PLACE"

God's will cannot be understood by logic or analysis. It is spiritually discerned as He reveals to us His secrets. By definition, a secret is: *something that is hidden, concealed, covered up and needs to be shared by the one who knows.* God knows and is fully willing to reveal His secrets to those who have hearts to hear, as follows:

Proverbs 3:32: Secret counsel.
32 For the perverse person is an abomination to the Lord, But His secret counsel is with the upright.

Deuteronomy 29:29: Reveals His secret things (which are His) to us.
29 The secret things belong to the Lord our God, but those things which are revealed belong to us and to our children forever, that we may do all the words of this law.

Psalm 25:14: Secrets revealed for those surrendered.
14 The secret of the Lord is with those who fear Him, And He will show them His covenant.

God has secrets to share with those who are willing to hear. The simple condition is for us to be abiding–walking with Him in the Spirit, fearing Him, surrendered to Him. We are not to rely on our own thinking or logical cause-and-effect, but rather to realize that God will reveal the secrets of His will to us through the Holy Spirit who is residing within us. As we ask, seek and knock we remain in a place for revelation (that which cannot be discerned naturally) to be given to us.

Psalm 91:1; 14-16: Place of answers.

1 He who dwells in the secret place of the Most High shall abide under the shadow of the Almighty.... 14 "Because he has set his love upon Me, therefore I will deliver him; I will set him on high, because he has known My name. 15 He shall call upon Me, and I will answer him; I will be with him in trouble; I will deliver him and honor him. 16 With long life I will satisfy him, And show him My salvation."

The secret place of the most high is Himself. We are called to abide in the secret place—as we discussed in chapter 8, abiding is being connected to the Vine—abiding in His word, hearing His voice, dialoguing with Him through prayer and walking connected in the Spirit. As we abide in this secret place, we can ask any and all questions and He will answer and deliver us from all trouble (things that distress us or are difficult for us). We will discover His will in the secret place and we will be satisfied—fulfilled.

Daniel 2:16-23; 30; 47; 4:9: Reveal deep things unknowable to us.

2:16 So Daniel went in and asked the king to give him time, that he might tell the king the interpretation. 17 Then Daniel went to his house, and made the decision known to Hananiah, Mishael, and Azariah, his companions, 18 that they might seek mercies from the God of heaven concerning this secret, so that Daniel and his companions might not perish with the rest of the wise men of Babylon. 19 Then the secret was revealed to Daniel in a night vision. So Daniel blessed the God of heaven. 20 Daniel answered and said: "Blessed be the name of God forever and ever, For wisdom and might are His. 21 And He changes the times and the seasons; He removes kings and raises up kings; He gives wisdom to the wise And knowledge to those who have understanding. 22 He reveals deep and secret things; He knows what is in the darkness, And light dwells with Him. 23 "I thank You and praise You, O God of my fathers; You have given me wisdom and might, And have now made known to me what we asked of You, For You have made known to us the king's demand."... 30 But as for me, this secret has not been revealed to me because I have more wisdom than anyone living, but for our sakes who make known the interpretation to the king, and that you may know the thoughts of your heart.... 47 The king answered Daniel, and said, "Truly your God is the God of gods, the Lord of kings, and a revealer of secrets, since you could reveal this secret."

4:9 "Belteshazzar, chief of the magicians, because I know that the Spirit of the Holy God is in you, and no secret troubles you, explain to me the visions of my dream that I have seen, and its interpretation.

In the secret place, Daniel asked for God to reveal secrets to him, and He did. Daniel recognized a very important element of this process—the secrets were not revealed to him because he was someone special or that he had more skill than anyone else; rather, he simply asked and expected God to reveal the secrets that no one could know except Him. He realized that he was privileged because he was a child of God and could fully receive the privilege of the secrets because of this intimate relationship. God is not prejudiced or only gives secrets to special people; rather, He offers these gifts to all who seek them.

Amos 3:1-8: God reveals His secrets to His children.

1 Hear this word that the Lord has spoken against you, O children of Israel, against the whole family which I brought up from the land of Egypt, saying: 2 "You only have I known of all the families of the earth; Therefore I will punish you for all your iniquities." 3 Can two walk together, unless they are agreed? 4 Will a lion roar in the forest, when he has no prey? Will a young lion cry out of his den, if he has caught nothing? 5 Will a bird fall into a snare on the earth, where there is no trap for it? Will a snare spring up from the earth, if it has caught nothing at all? 6 If a trumpet is blown in a city, will not the people be afraid? If there is calamity in a city, will not the Lord have done it? 7 Surely the Lord God does nothing, unless He reveals His secret to His servants the prophets. 8 A lion has roared! Who will not fear? The Lord God has spoken! Who can but prophesy?

God's ways are not our ways and His thoughts are not our thoughts. He first reveals His secrets to those of His servants who are willing to hear. Inherent in this process is our prophetic place, which is to hear and then speak what we hear–in other words, share His secrets that are being given to us. His will becomes clear to us and with great confidence we can then declare it. What we are told in secret is to be declared publicly.

That is why part of the definition of hearing His will is that: It is so clear that we can in fact confidently declare it to others. He wants us to not be so afraid of what we hear in secret that we hesitate to speak it. We are to realize that much of what the Lord speaks to us will be interesting, but not seem natural or so logical. He wants to reveal to us amazing truths and amazing steps that are known to Him but unknown to us. It is a privilege to hear and then to declare. May we all be open to this process of receiving His secrets.

HIS SECRETS ARE REVEALED THROUGH HIM SPEAKING AND US HEARING:

Since it is clear that His heart is to reveal secrets to us that will guide us into His will, we must fully understand that He speaks secrets and we are to hear the secrets. This is a key role of the Holy Spirit, who is resident within us.

John 16:13-15: Spirit's job.

13 However, when He, the Spirit of truth, has come, He will guide you into all truth; for He will not speak on His own authority, but whatever He hears He will speak; and He will tell you things to come. 14 He will glorify Me, for He will take of what is Mine and declare it to you. 15 All things that the Father has are Mine. Therefore I said that He will take of Mine and declare it to you.

His role is to guide us into all truth (not just theological truth, but all truth about our circumstances, our heart and response to circumstances, our emotions, our understanding, and then His truth that He

117

desires us to hear, receive, understand and follow). He also is to tell us of things to come—foretelling what is ahead. This normally alerts us to things to pay attention to. Further, His job is to transfer all that is Christ's to you. Christ is living in the resurrection where all has been given Him. He wants to give us the abundant life here and now. The Holy Spirit is to be the transfer agent of this. It happens through abiding. The Spirit recognizes that it is His role to adapt His communication and way of guiding us to what we can receive. All we have to do is have a heart to receive and pay attention to the guidance of the Holy Spirit into the truth of His will. This means being sensitive to information, confirmation and the Spirit giving us peace or checking our spirit as we are seeking this truth.

Isaiah 30:18-26: Speak specifics, at right moment will be very detailed.

18 Therefore the Lord will wait, that He may be gracious to you; And therefore He will be exalted, that He may have mercy on you. For the Lord is a God of justice; Blessed are all those who wait for Him. 19 For the people shall dwell in Zion at Jerusalem; You shall weep no more. He will be very gracious to you at the sound of your cry; When He hears it, He will answer you. 20 And though the Lord gives you The bread of adversity and the water of affliction, Yet your teachers will not be moved into a corner anymore, But your eyes shall see your teachers. 21 Your ears shall hear a word behind you, saying, "This is the way, walk in it," Whenever you turn to the right hand Or whenever you turn to the left. 22 You will also defile the covering of your graven images of silver, And the ornament of your molded images of gold. You will throw them away as an unclean thing; You will say to them, "Get away!" 23 Then He will give the rain for your seed With which you sow the ground, And bread of the increase of the earth; It will be fat and plentiful. In that day your cattle will feed In large pastures. 24 Likewise the oxen and the young donkeys that work the ground Will eat cured fodder, Which has been winnowed with the shovel and fan. 25 There will be on every high mountain And on every high hill Rivers and streams of waters, In the day of the great slaughter, When the towers fall. 26

Moreover the light of the moon will be as the light of the sun, And the light of the sun will be sevenfold, As the light of seven days, In the day that the Lord binds up the bruise of His people And heals the stroke of their wound.

God is waiting for us to surrender our lives and will to Him and be willing to hear what He has to speak to us. We then wait for the fulfillment of what He is speaking to us. As we call, He answers and speaks to us through the Spirit. We are no longer to put the Spirit in the corner–striving to walk the Christian life alone or studying the Bible on our own in the shallowness of our own intellect (or not at all). Rather, we are to allow the Spirit to lead us step-by-step. He will tell us whether to turn to the right or to the left (very directly and specifically). In this description He refers to speaking from behind–implying that we are not to rely on our senses (what we can see, hear and understand with our limited logic), but rather to just listen and follow. If I told someone that I was going to blindfold them and walk them to their car, he or she would have to listen completely and take the steps that I speak (because I know the way and he or she does not). Same with the Holy Spirit–we must hear His voice and be led, step-by-step into the wonderful plans of giving us the abundant life that God has prepared in advance for us. Why would we not?

♦ Example: Saul, Ananias: Acts 9:1-19:

1 Then Saul, still breathing threats and murder against the disciples of the Lord, went to the high priest 2 and asked letters from him to the synagogues of Damascus, so that if he found any who were of the Way, whether men or women, he might bring them bound to Jerusalem. 3 As he journeyed he came near Damascus, and suddenly a light shone around him from heaven. 4 Then he fell to the ground, and heard a voice saying to him, "Saul, Saul, why are you persecuting Me?" 5 And he said, "Who are You, Lord?" Then the Lord said, "I am Jesus, whom you are persecuting. 6 So he, trembling and astonished, said, "Lord, what do You want me to do?" Then the Lord said to him, "Arise and go into the city, and you will be told what you must do." 7 And the men who journeyed with him stood speechless, hearing a voice but seeing no one. 8 Then Saul arose from the ground, and when his eyes were opened he saw no one. But they led him by the hand and brought him into Damascus. 9 And he was three days without sight, and neither ate nor drank. 10 Now there was a certain disciple at Damascus named Ananias; and to him the Lord said in a vision, "Ananias." And he said, "Here I am, Lord." 11 So the Lord said to him, "Arise and go to the street called Straight, and inquire at the house of Judas for one called Saul of Tarsus, for behold, he is praying. 12 And in a vision he has seen a man named Ananias coming in and putting his hand on him, so that he might receive his sight." 13 Then Ananias answered, "Lord, I have heard from many about this man, how much harm he has done to Your saints in Jerusalem. 14 And here he has authority from the chief priests to bind all who call on Your name." 15 But the Lord said to him, "Go, for he is a chosen vessel of Mine to bear My name before Gentiles, kings, and the children of Israel. 16 For I will show him how many things he must suffer for My name's sake." 17 And Ananias went his way and entered the house; and laying his hands on him he said, "Brother Saul, the Lord Jesus, who appeared to you on the road as you came, has sent me that you may receive your sight and be filled with the Holy Spirit." 18 Immediately there fell from his eyes something like scales, and he received his sight at once; and he arose and was baptized. 19 So when he had received food, he was strengthened. Then Saul spent some days with the disciples at Damascus.

This is a wonderful story of God working His specific will through the work of the Holy Spirit. Most of us know the conversion story of Saul—as he was on the way to Damascus to track down and arrest Christians (whom he thought were speaking and working blasphemy against the Jewish beliefs). Christ appeared to him and he was struck blind. He was instructed by Christ to go into the city and wait until he was told what to do next. Then the Holy Spirit spoke to Ananias, who was told to go to a specific street and a specific house and lay hands on Saul (Paul). Ananias resisted this assignment since he knew that Paul was the one who was chasing and persecuting Christians; so he desired clarification about God's will since it did not make any sense to him.

The Lord does not mind this intimate dialogue and did confirm that yes, that was his assignment and actually revealed two big secrets: (1) that Paul had received a vision from the Spirit that a man called Ananias would come and lay hands on him so he might receive his sight–both physically and spiritually, and (2) that Paul would open up the Gospel to the Gentiles. This was the first time that anyone had heard this specific secret truth. With this confirmation, and with the specifics given of exactly where to go, Ananias went to the specific street to the specific house and laid hands on Paul who did receive his sight and accepted Christ as his Lord and Savior. God worked both sides of His will–getting the right people in the right spot at the right time.

He spoke specifically to Paul, and He spoke specifically to Ananias. Both had hearts to hear, received His secret will and then followed His instructions so that His will would be fulfilled. We can expect the same in our lives–how beautiful is this?

Psalm 18:28-33: Give light, see clearly, makes my way perfect (His way).

28 For You will light my lamp; The Lord my God will enlighten my darkness. 29 For by You I can run against a troop, By my God I can leap over a wall. 30 As for God, His way is perfect; The word of the Lord is proven; He is a shield to all who trust in Him. 31 For who is God, except the Lord? And who is a rock, except our God? 32 It is God who arms me with strength, And makes my way perfect. 33 He makes my feet like the feet of deer, And sets me on my high places.

As we are pursuing God's will and trying to understand His secrets, things are often fuzzy and not clear (being in darkness). The Lord promises to give light and clarity so that things that are dark become known and understandable. His way is perfect and He promises to make my way perfect, too. It is not through Him blessing my way, but rather me joining Him on His perfect way, which then by definition makes our way perfect as well. We have to trust the light and the insight that He is bringing and continue to walk in that light based on the clarity that He brings.

Ezekiel 12:25-28: Word that He has spoken will be done.

25 It will come to pass when you come to the land, which the Lord will give you, just as He promised, that you shall keep this service. 26 And it shall be, when your children say to you, 'What do you mean by this service?' 27 that you shall say, 'It is the Passover sacrifice of the Lord, who passed over the houses of the children of Israel in Egypt when He struck the Egyptians and delivered our households.' So the people bowed their heads and worshiped. 28 Then the children of Israel went away and did so; just as the Lord had commanded Moses and Aaron, so they did.

God says over and over again that what He speaks will be done. We can have confidence that God's desire when He speaks is to perform what He says, and thus there is never a question on His part that what He says will be performed. We can thus be assured that He does not change His mind nor arbitrarily bait and switch us. We need to learn that whatever He speaks is truly ready to be performed for us. This is an important concept to hammer home so that there is never doubt about the integrity and follow-through of God.

Our role is to hear what He has spoken and then walk with Him as He moves us to belief in what He has spoken—and then expect it to be done. As we stated before, His will is primarily what He wishes to do for us, and our instructions are just to be able to get to the right place with the right people at the right time—joining Him in His work. Our response is really simple—Amen: so be it.

Isaiah 55:8-13: Not our ways or thoughts—be willing to be surprised and amazed.

8 "For My thoughts are not your thoughts, Nor are your ways My ways," says the Lord. 9 "For as the heavens are higher than the earth, So are My ways higher than your ways, And My thoughts than your thoughts. 10 "For as the rain comes down, and the snow from heaven, And do not re-

turn there, But water the earth, And make it bring forth and bud, That it may give seed to the sower And bread to the eater, 11 So shall My word be that goes forth from My mouth; It shall not return to Me void, But it shall accomplish what I please, And it shall prosper in the thing for which I sent it. 12 "For you shall go out with joy, And be led out with peace; The mountains and the hills Shall break forth into singing before you, And all the trees of the field shall clap their hands. 13 Instead of the thorn shall come up the cypress tree, And instead of the brier shall come up the myrtle tree; And it shall be to the Lord for a name, For an everlasting sign that shall not be cut off."*

God's ways and thoughts are not our ways and thoughts. Thus, we are not to view the resolution to our circumstances in light of how we would resolve them. God's ways and thoughts are so much broader and bigger than ours that we are simply to listen to what He speaks without judging whether it makes sense to us or not. This is important as we are reviewing His promises since often the promises given will be so grand or so big that it will be hard for us to see the possibility of them.

Further, we are not to apply logic or natural cause-and-effect to what He says, but rather just to receive what He says. It does not have to make sense to us, and thus our focus should be strictly on hearing and clarifying, not on evaluating. Again, God says His word will not return void and that what He speaks will come to pass. This is another reminder that we can have every confidence in His promises turning into reality. Since His ways are not our ways, we are called to not judge the validity of His ways and instructions–rather to receive and understand that they will be secrets and can be trusted.

Isaiah 14:24-27: Who can annul it? No one except us.

24 The Lord of hosts has sworn, saying, "Surely, as I have thought, so it shall come to pass, And as I have purposed, so it shall stand: 25 That I will break the Assyrian in My land, And on My mountains tread him underfoot. Then his yoke shall be removed from them, And his burden removed from their shoulders. 26 This is the purpose that is purposed against the whole earth, And this is the hand that is stretched out over all the nations. 27 For the Lord of hosts has purposed, And who will annul it? His hand is stretched out, And who will turn it back?"

God's word will stand, and He asks the question, "Who can annul it?" We would assume nothing and nobody. There is no force, no circumstance and no other person that can annul what God speaks–but there is only one who can annul it–us!

Circumstances, Satan, principalities and powers–none of these can annul it–only us. Since everything that God speaks has potential and is not guaranteed, we can annul it by not hearing it, not following Him, not abiding and moving in the flesh on our own. He invites us to His spectacular will, but does require us to have a heart to hear or to follow. We will explore in the next chapter some of the ways we can annul His will.

Romans 10:17: Faith comes by hearing, hearing by the Word (Rhema).

17 So then faith comes by hearing, and hearing by the word of God.

We are called to faith–certainly what God has spoken to us is true and will be performed. As we hear His promises, we usually struggle with how grand and wonderful they are for us in our particular circumstances. The Lord understands that it is a process. Our only requirement is to receive the faith that comes from Him by hearing and then abiding in His word until it becomes faith. This is where journaling and processing is so critical as we understand where our doubts come from or where we struggle, and how He can speak to our hearts and persuade us until we get to faith.

The process of hearing is very simple: give attention to, consider and ponder what is being said, seek to understand, and gain clarity about what He has spoken personally to us. It is a joy to hear, and that is where faith comes from. We are called to stay with it and continue to process until His will is known and we believe what He said will be done.

In His Kingdom:
Matthew 18:3-5; 19:14: Entered and experienced as a little child.

18:3 and said, "Assuredly, I say to you, unless you are converted and become as little children, you will by no means enter the kingdom of heaven. 4 Therefore whoever humbles himself as this little child is the greatest in the kingdom of heaven. 5 Whoever receives one little child like this in My name receives Me.

19:14 But Jesus said, "Let the little children come to Me, and do not forbid them; for of such is the kingdom of heaven."

His will is carried out in His kingdom. He is the King, and thus we enter the kingdom surrendered to the King as a little child. We desire His will, seek His will and have a heart to hear and follow His will. A child does not resist or neglect the will of the Father. They are excited to carry out the will of the Father, knowing the likelihood of the gifts the Father will deliver to them. God wants us to live the life of a child in His kingdom.

Mark 10:14-16: Choices we are to make.
14 But when Jesus saw it, He was greatly displeased and said to them, "Let the little children come to Me, and do not forbid them; for of such is the kingdom of God. 15 Assuredly, I say to you, whoever does not receive the kingdom of God as a little child will by no means enter it." 16 And He took them up in His arms, put His hands on them, and blessed them.

We are called to receive the kingdom of God so that we can enter into that place. It is our choice–are we willing to surrender to the King with a willing heart, to hear and follow? The simple choice is that we will enter in and be in that place where He can fulfill His will.

Requires Discernment:

Because His secrets are not known through logic and natural thinking, we must have spiritual discernment. It takes sensitivity to the work of the Holy Spirit within us that gives us this discernment:

1 Kings 3:5-9: Hearing heart.

5 At Gibeon the Lord appeared to Solomon in a dream by night; and God said, "Ask! What shall I give you?" 6 And Solomon said: "You have shown great mercy to Your servant David my father, because he walked before You in truth, in righteousness, and in uprightness of heart with You; You have continued this great kindness for him, and You have given him a son to sit on his throne, as it is this day. 7 Now, O Lord my God, You have made Your servant king instead of my father David, but I am a little child; I do not know how to go out or come in. 8 And Your servant is in the midst of Your people whom You have chosen, a great people, too numerous to be numbered or counted. 9 Therefore give to Your servant an understanding heart to judge Your people, that I may discern between good and evil. For who is able to judge this great people of Yours?"

When God came to Solomon and asked him what he wanted, he stated three important things:

1. He understood that he was like a little kid that did not know answers or presume to have great wisdom. He admitted that he needed to know God's will, but that he couldn't determine that on his own or just act on his own.

2. Based upon this, Solomon asked for an understanding heart. This Hebrew word means: hearing, listening with a heart to agree. He asked for a heart to hear, to be able to receive and understand God's secret so that he could have clarity regarding His will.

3. The purpose of having a hearing heart is to have discernment between good and evil. The word "evil" here is not what we normally think. There is not much discernment needed between white and black, good and awful. What we need discernment for is the gray–what looks good to us but in fact is evil; what is going to turn out to be frustrating, distracting, difficult, oppressive, irritating and hard.

We often can see things as good for us that actually turn out to be evil. This is why God's will is about His secrets and the truth being revealed to us. We need to understand the difference between good (i.e. what He considers to be wonderful according to His will) and what will not be so good.

We have to approach it as Solomon did. Come with a heart without pride and seek His will because He knows and we don't. Ask for a hearing heart then receive the discernment that will lead us to understanding the difference between good and evil.

Hebrews 5:14: Use all our senses–practice it.
14 But solid food belongs to those who are of full age, that is, those who by reason of use have their senses exercised to discern both good and evil.

As we desire to receive discernment, we are encouraged to actually use all of senses together to receive His discernment. Thus, we are to pay attention to our thinking, our feeling, our spiritual understanding, etc. They should all be used together to get us to a place of understanding and clarity. If we have not yet received or understood His will, He will cause a troubling and an unsettling feeling so that we continue to move forward until we reach clarity. We are to enjoy using all of our senses together.

Requires Prophetic:
As we process God secrets through hearing hearts and receiving discernment, we are given the gift of the prophetic–which means:

1. Forth-telling–the truth that God wishes to speak into any situation.

2. Fore-telling–insight as to what is ahead.

This is the work of the Holy Spirit and is available to us all. As we grow in our spiritual discernment, we will grow in this gift of the prophetic.

Ephesians 1:15-21: Spirit of wisdom and revelation, supernatural.

15 Therefore I also, after I heard of your faith in the Lord Jesus and your love for all the saints, 16 do not cease to give thanks for you, making mention of you in my prayers: 17 that the God of our Lord Jesus Christ, the Father of glory, may give to you the spirit of wisdom and revelation in the knowledge of Him, 18 the eyes of your understanding being enlightened; that you may know what is the hope of His calling, what are the riches of the glory of His inheritance in the saints, 19 and what is the exceeding greatness of His power toward us who believe, according to the working of His mighty power 20 which He worked in Christ when He raised Him from the dead and seated Him at His right hand in the heavenly places, 21 far above all principality and power and might and dominion.

Paul urges us to pray by asking for the prophetic spirit–specifically ask for:

1. wisdom: manage affairs with God's perspective, interpret things spiritual;

2. revelation: disclosing things not known naturally, laying open, laying bare;

3. knowledge: correct truth;

4. understanding: thoughts and emotions (heart, soul) getting it;

5. enlighten: give light, clarity;

6. hope: confident and expectation;

7. calling: invitation to feast;

8. riches: wealth;

9. honor: dignity, riches, abundance;

10. glory: splendor, beauty;

11. inheritance: His possession;

12. power: (dunamis) authority (against circumstances and spiritual powers);

13. toward us: ours to have;

14. power: external force, might, to make circumstances change;

15. power: (exousia)–governing power;

As we ask for this spiritual capability, He will give us the following:

1. Wisdom and revelation (things disclosed only by Him) to help us carry out the practical things and decisions of life;

2. Understanding (wisdom and revelation are not to be mechanical but to be understood relative to His grander and eternal purposes–driving us into His bigger story);

3. Knowing that the hope of our calling is to be invited to His great feast, and thus it is more about what He wishes to do and not about us working for Him;

4. Knowing that we are His inheritance as we die to self and gain fellowship back with Him so that He enjoys being with us;

5. That His supernatural power is planned to be given to us in our everyday circumstances.

We are to pray, pray, pray–ask Him for the special gift and expect it.

Jeremiah 33:3: Great and mighty things we could never know.

3 'Call to Me, and I will answer you, and show you great and mighty things, which you do not know.'

God issues another invitation to simply call out to Him as we seek to hear His secrets. He promises to answer with great and mighty things that we could never know by ourselves. These great things will be powerful and things that we cannot understand, discern, observe, perceive, discover or comprehend on our own power. They are unknowable other than through the prophetic gift of the Holy Spirit that is promised by God.

We are to pray, pray, pray–ask Him to reveal great and mighty things that we do not know and expect it.

1 Corinthians 14 1-3; Romans 12:6: Instructive, encouraging, comforting.

1 Corinthians 14:1 Pursue love, and desire spiritual gifts, but especially that you may prophesy. 2 For he who speaks in a tongue does not speak to men but to God, for no one understands him; however, in the spirit he speaks mysteries. 3 But he who prophesies speaks edification and exhortation and comfort to men.

Romans 12:6 Having then gifts differing according to the grace that is given to us, let us use them: if prophecy, let us prophesy in proportion to our faith;

God's prophetic gift is always comforting, edifying and instructive. Since His desire is to take us along the good path of covenant blessing, His prophecy is always encouraging—even when it is asking us to repent and turn from where we are headed. It may reveal some difficulties ahead, but based on His promises, we will work through the difficulty, and safely reach the other side.

We are to desire this and realize that God wishes to convey to us the prophetic understanding of truth and what is ahead. This aids us in the process of understanding His will. We are to pay attention to our impressions, to words from other people, to insights, to revelation that clarifies and gives understanding of His will. Remember it is not naturally known but is through the secret gift of the prophetic that it will be discovered.

2 Peter 1:16-21: Open for confirmation, not private interpretation.

16 For we did not follow cunningly devised fables when we made known to you the power and coming of our Lord Jesus Christ, but were eyewitnesses of His majesty. 17 For He received from God the Father honor and glory when such a voice came to Him from the Excellent Glory: "This is My beloved Son, in whom I am well pleased." 18 And we heard this voice which came from heaven when we were with Him on the holy mountain. 19 And so we have the prophetic word confirmed, which you do well to heed as a light that shines in a dark place, until the day dawns and the morning star rises in your hearts; 20 knowing this first, that no prophecy of Scripture is of any private interpretation, 21 for prophecy never came by the will of man, but holy men of Godc spoke as they were moved by the Holy Spirit.

It is important to note that the prophetic is never to be subject to private interpretation. God uses others in the body—especially our spouses or those in our inner circle to confirm the prophetic. Since we are seeking wisdom and revelation, we never should be afraid to discuss openly what we are hearing in secret. This helps us avoid the problems of both over-interpretation and under-interpretation. Others have the same Holy Spirit that we do and have the same gifts of the prophetic.

Thus, God encourages us to openly discuss what we are receiving prophetically so that He can help to instruct and clarify exactly what He is saying. Often, we apply the prophetic to more specific detail than is spoken. If we are pure and just share what is spoken, others can help us see that it is being spoken to guide us down the path without giving us the full path. It is a true joy to have confirmation from others and to openly discuss what each of us is hearing prophetically. It can keep us on the right path and help us follow the instructions given.

Joel 2:28-30: Dreams and visions–receive and expect.

28 "And it shall come to pass afterward That I will pour out My Spirit on all flesh; Your sons and your daughters shall prophesy, Your old men shall dream dreams, Your young men shall see visions. 29 And also on My menservants and on My maidservants I will pour out My Spirit in those days. 30 "And I will show wonders in the heavens and in the earth: Blood and fire and pillars of smoke.

Important elements of the prophetic our dreams and visions.

As we are seeking God's will, He will use dreams and visions to give us pictures and important revelations. Dreams are rarely to be interpreted as specific instructions. The imagery of people, places and things are generally not specifically those places, people or things–rather, representations of messages that God wishes to convey to us. They are important messages though–and are usually very simple to receive. I suggest that you keep a journal by your bed and, as you wake up from a dream, write down all the specific detail that you can immediately remember. We often think that when we awake in the morning we will still fully remember our vivid dream, but rarely do. That is why it is important to write out the detail at the time of the dream.

When you awake in the morning, ask the Father to reveal the message of the dream. The message will be spiritually discerned and again is very simple to interpret, including a warning or a rebuke. Again this is where opening up to public interpretation is helpful. Share the dream with your spouse or with a good friend and ask if they have insight as to the meaning. The more that you seek the meaning the more likely you are to receive the meaning. God has a message and uses dreams and visions to communicate that message. Pay attention and then ask for further clarification as to the importance of these messages and what exactly He is using this for in expressing His will to us. It is a beautiful way to receive discernment and insight.

Psalm 16:7: Happens while we sleep.
7 I will bless the Lord who has given me counsel; My heart also instructs me in the night seasons.

In addition to dreams and visions, He can just speak to us during the night season. This is particularly effective since our conscious is asleep and not in the way. Our reasoning does not take over so we are able to receive His instruction. It is important to realize how precious this is. As we ponder His will and abide in His word, it is good to go to bed with His word and to wake up with His word.

I do this through memory of the words He is speaking to me, and I pray these verses asking for clarity, understanding, wisdom and application. When I wake up, I do the same. Often, I will be woken up in the middle of night with an insight or an understanding–another reason why I keep a journal by the bed. Furthermore, my soul is being enlightened so that as I ask, seek, knock and listen, watch, and wait, the insight given during the night season can give the secrets that I might not otherwise know. It is a precious gift and a very exciting gift.

Example: 2 Chronicles 20:1-30 Jehoshaphat
1 It happened after this that the people of Moab with the people of Ammon, and others with them besides the Ammonites, came to battle against Jehoshaphat. 2 Then some came and told Jehoshaphat, saying, "A great multitude is coming against you from beyond the sea, from Syria; and they are in Hazazon Tamar" (which is En Gedi). 3 And Jehoshaphat feared, and set himself to seek the Lord, and proclaimed a fast throughout all Judah. 4 So Judah gathered together to ask help from the Lord; and from all

the cities of Judah they came to seek the Lord. 5 Then Jehoshaphat stood in the assembly of Judah and Jerusalem, in the house of the Lord, before the new court, 6 and said: "O Lord God of our fathers, are You not God in heaven, and do You not rule over all the kingdoms of the nations, and in Your hand is there not power and might, so that no one is able to withstand You? 7 Are You not our God, who drove out the inhabitants of this land before Your people Israel, and gave it to the descendants of Abraham Your friend forever? 8 And they dwell in it, and have built You a sanctuary in it for Your name, saying, 9 'If disaster comes upon us—sword, judgment, pestilence, or famine—we will stand before this temple and in Your presence (for Your name is in this temple), and cry out to You in our affliction, and You will hear and save.' 10 And now, here are the people of Ammon, Moab, and Mount Seir—whom You would not let Israel invade when they came out of the land of Egypt, but they turned from them and did not destroy them— 11 here they are, rewarding us by coming to throw us out of Your possession which You have given us to inherit. 12 O our God, will You not judge them? For we have no power against this great multitude that is coming against us; nor do we know what to do, but our eyes are upon You." 13 Now all Judah, with their little ones, their wives, and their children, stood before the Lord. 14 Then the Spirit of the Lord came upon Jahaziel the son of Zechariah, the son of Benaiah, the son of Jeiel, the son of Mattaniah, a Levite of the sons of Asaph, in the midst of the assembly. 15 And he said, "Listen, all you of Judah and you inhabitants of Jerusalem, and you, King Jehoshaphat! Thus says the Lord to you: 'Do not be afraid nor dismayed because of this great multitude, for the battle is not yours, but God's. 16 Tomorrow go down against them. They will surely come up by the Ascent of Ziz, and you will find them at the end of the brook before the Wilderness of Jeruel. 17 You will not need to fight in this battle. Position yourselves, stand still and see the salvation of the Lord, who is with you, O Judah and Jerusalem!' Do not fear or be dismayed; tomorrow go out against them, for the Lord is with you." 18 And Jehoshaphat bowed his head with his face to the ground, and all Judah and the inhabitants of Jerusalem bowed before the Lord, worshiping the Lord. 19 Then the Levites of the children of the Kohathites and of the children of the Korahites stood up to praise the Lord God of Israel with voices loud and high. 20 So they rose early in the morning and went out into the Wilderness of Tekoa; and as they went out, Jehoshaphat stood and said, "Hear me, O Judah and you inhabitants of Jerusalem: Believe in the Lord your God, and you shall be established; believe His prophets, and you shall prosper." 21 And when he had consulted with the people, he appointed those who should sing to the Lord, and who should praise the beauty of holiness, as they went out before the army and were saying: "Praise the Lord, For His mercy endures forever." 22 Now when they began to sing and to praise, the Lord set ambushes against the people of Ammon, Moab, and Mount Seir, who had come against Judah; and they were defeated. 23 For the people of Ammon and Moab stood up against the inhabitants of Mount Seir to utterly kill and destroy them. And when they had made an end of the inhabitants of Seir, they helped to destroy one another. 24 So when Judah came to a place overlooking the wilderness, they looked toward the multitude; and there were their dead bodies, fallen on the earth. No one had escaped. 25 When Jehoshaphat and his people came to take away their spoil, they found among them an abundance of valuables on the dead bodies, and precious jewelry, which they stripped off for themselves, more than they could carry away; and they were three days gathering the spoil because there was so much. 26 And on the fourth day they assembled in the Valley of Berachah, for there they blessed the Lord; therefore the name of that place was called The Valley of Berachah until this day. 27 Then they returned, every man of Judah and Jerusalem, with Jehoshaphat in front of them, to go back to Jerusalem with joy, for the Lord had made them rejoice over their enemies. 28 So they came to Jerusalem, with stringed instruments and harps and trumpets, to the house of the Lord. 29 And the fear of God was on all the kingdoms of those countries when they heard that the Lord had fought against the enemies of Israel. 30 Then the realm of Jehoshaphat was quiet, for his God gave him rest all around.

Jehoshaphat was faced with a problem much larger than he could solve on his own. War in those times were primarily won by numbers—the nation with the largest army usually won the battle by being able to overwhelm the opposition. In this case, three nations formed an alliance and came against Israel—there was no way in the natural that Israel might survive. So Jehoshaphat gathered the people together and went to prayer and fasting, seeking God's will. They did understand that God had made a promise to the nation of Israel that if they surrendered their will to God, He would deliver and preserve them.

During this time of seeking, they stood on this promise and admitted they had no idea as to how this might happen or what role they were to play. God spoke clearly–the battle was not theirs but His, and He would defeat the enemy. The role of the people was to go out to battle, sing praises (the choir was asked to go first) and watch God fulfill His promise. He spoke clearly of His work and the steps they were to take to receive His promise. It is a wonderful example of God responding with clarity to our seeking what to do in specific situations.

As discussed in our last chapter, our retreat ministry (Living Waters) had grown from once a year, weeklong retreats in Europe to six weekend retreats at our home in Colorado (in addition to the weeklong retreats in Europe, which we have done every year). The following year, the retreats grew to 10 and we were having more interest than Linda and I could manage. We knew that if we overdid it and served all the demand, we would lose the essence of our own sweet life as a couple and then would have nothing to offer anyone–an interesting enigma.

We continued to pray and seek the will of God, and He revealed to us a few secrets. He said we were to look for property to build a new retreat home, as our current home was experiencing stress and was not big enough for larger groups. (Our retreats generally included three to six couples, so larger was going from four to six.) The Father told us to get ready, as the ministry was going to expand rapidly, and to give it priority. As we processed what this meant further, it was clear that though we had other involvements and had other gifts in ministry, we were to give this our sole priority. Interestingly, as soon as we had the secret revealed to us, I had numerous requests from multiple ministries to get involved with their wonderful activity.

I certainly had the capability and the heart, but because God had given us his prophetic message, we knew that we were to leave open the upcoming growth of the ministry and to give it our full attention– while maintaining our own margin in life and the relaxed pace that we had come to enjoy. We did establish an official 501-C3 ministry organization. Up until now, we and our family had funded all the cost, as we never charged anybody for the retreats (except for the European retreats, where we share the expenses), which were always conducted with first-class, gourmet food, etc. Many people had offered to assist but we had no place to which they could donate.

As we expanded down the road, this became important as many people wanted to contribute to the ministry and provided the funds for retreats that are conducted all over the country. We never asked anyone for funding and we never had a shortage of funds. God always met His needs, as all funding went directly to expenses and none to overhead or staff. We were all volunteers.

Having been given instruction to find property, I would have, in the past, acted immediately and found something based upon my own analysis of what worked. Having learned that my role was strictly to follow God's direction, I waited until he showed us His will. One day, while we were driving around with our daughter near her new home, we noticed a sign that said "35 acres for sale." The property was beautiful and had a 360° view (actually, the very highest point in Castle Rock), and asked the Father if we were to pursue this. He said, "Yes." We did, and were informed by the broker that though the property had been sitting for a year, someone had just purchased it the day before. We had heard God clearly, so did not know what this all meant.

Our daughter said that she was glad we didn't get it because she liked the property next to it much better. I told her that it was not for sale. She asked how I was so sure. In Colorado, we can actually look up the tax records of the owner with their phone number, so I called the owner and stated that we had missed out on the property next to him and asked if his property was available. He said that actually, he and his wife were considering it and that they would be interested in talking. So we met, and I said that I'd be willing to pay the same price as the price of the lot next door, and they agreed. We signed a contract.

During due diligence, the owner called and said he had to meet. He said that he had to confess that he knew some information that was important for our consideration, and that he would rather not sell the property at this time. The county was considering building a road through the lot adjacent to this on the other side, and thus might cause the value of his property to drop. We, again, had hit a roadblock, so we just continued to pray. The Father told us to go to the county and find out for ourselves. So I did, and they told us that, though it was not public that they had discarded that lot as the one that they were to build the road through, they would put it in writing. With that letter I went back to the seller and we concluded our transaction. We had God's place for the ministry!

During the next year of construction, we continued to grow the ministry and we were conducting 14 per year in addition to the European retreats. After a year in our new retreat home, we were still conducting 14 per year plus Europe, and the interest from other couples who wanted to come to the retreats was higher than we could receive. We continued to seek God's will, and He told us that we were to shift from us doing all the retreats to building leaders and multiplying.

Linda and I shifted, and began inviting couples that had attended previous retreats to attend second and third retreats and be trained as leaders. This further meant that we had to slough other activities, as this now was occupying even more of our time and we never wanted to lose the sweetness of our marriage and family, nor the joy of ministry. (Note, I never understood people in ministry who are miserable because of the workload—means something is not right; Christ is our model and always had a paced life and great joy!)

A few years later, we now have 20 couples who are leading retreats around the country, with more leaders on the way. All of us are volunteers and realize that our role is to maintain our intimate relationship with Christ through abiding in the Vine and then "giving it away." If it were not for the secrets given to us by God and His prophetic messages to us, we would have developed this ministry in the flesh and developed great programs that likely would have little impact in reality. We certainly would not have experienced the miraculous work of God through all these years, nor would those who had attended the retreats.

God's will is not just about what we do; rather, it is about what He does and wants to do. And He always leads us to his supernatural work, and the thrill of it is beyond description. We are always called to a bigger story, and it is always going to be best and none better. Why would anyone want anything different?

13

ALWAYS BE WILLING TO RECEIVE NEW INFORMATION, INTERPRET CIRCUMSTANCES AND NEW INSTRUCTION–PROCESS, PROCESS, PROCESS

As we have described the process of seeking His will through asking, seeking and knocking; having a hearing heart and receiving secrets; being open to the prophetic gifts and messages from God, one thing is important–always be willing to receive new information, reinterpret circumstances and new instruction. The key is processing, processing, processing. As we seek wisdom, He promises to communicate His will. We are to expect it. It is a step-by-step process, and not to be seen as a final answer coming to us all at once. Rather it is progressive–piece-by-piece and step-by-step. Thus, as we are moving step-by-step and receiving progressive revelation, we are always to be open to the things that He does today to clarify His will.

Acts 16:6-12: Cooperate with God blocking things.

6 Now when they had gone through Phrygia and the region of Galatia, they were forbidden by the Holy Spirit to preach the word in Asia. 7 After they had come to Mysia, they tried to go into Bithynia, but the Spirit did not permit them. 8 So passing by Mysia, they came down to Troas. 9 And a vision appeared to Paul in the night. A man of Macedonia stood and pleaded with him, saying, "Come over to Macedonia and help us." 10 Now after he had seen the vision, immediately we sought to go to Macedonia, concluding that the Lord had called us to preach the gospel to them. 11 Therefore, sailing from Troas, we ran a straight course to Samothrace, and the next day came to Neapolis, 12 and from there to Philippi, which is the foremost city of that part of Macedonia, a colony. And we were staying in that city for some days.

Paul understood the path of God's will—to serve as a missionary by going from city to city and discipling a group of elders who would start and lead churches. After Paul had gone through the region of Phrygia and Galatia, he had a desire to spread the word in Asia, which was east. However, he was forbidden by the Holy Spirit. He had received prophetic insight that God was saying "no." After they had gone further to Mysia, they thought it a good idea to go north to spread the word, but the Spirit again did not permit them to go. In some way he was continually blocked, either through a troubling of the Spirit or through circumstances that did not allow him to proceed.

He was at a place where the Mediterranean Sea was south and west. It appeared that he was stuck and did not know where to go next. He was blocked from going east, and he was blocked from going north, and could not go west or south. The key here is that he did not overrule the work of the Spirit by deciding on his own that it would be good to go north or east since it made the most sense. Rather, he received the prophetic work of the Spirit and waited for further instruction. He received it through a vision of a man from Macedonia (Philippi) who asked him to come there to spread the word. Paul realized that this was his next instruction and left for Philippi.

It should be noted that he traveled through other cities on the way to Philippi but did not stop to start churches there. He understood God's will was specific to Philippi and fully followed His instructions. He fully cooperated with God blocking him and then showing him the specifics of His will.

Further, though Paul heard God's voice, he did not rely on any past experience of understanding God's will. In this situation, God used a different way of working through circumstances to direct him. Paul never moved into a system, but rather received God's fresh way of communicating His will.

Proverbs 8:32-35: Listen, watch, wait–pay attention to new data.

32 "Now therefore, listen to me, my children, For blessed are those who keep my ways. 33 Hear instruction and be wise, And do not disdain it. 34 Blessed is the man who listens to me, Watching daily at my gates, Waiting at the posts of my doors. 35 For whoever finds me finds life, And obtains favor from the Lord;

As we are called to hear His instruction, He tells us specifically to follow the steps as we receive new information:

1. Listen: hears, yield to obey, be obedient

2. Watch: be alert, observe new data

3. Wait: keep, guard, do not make decision until clear

He will continue to speak new things, so receive by listening and paying attention; we are to watch for interesting things that happen and new information that comes to us. Always pay attention to what is next and what things are brought to us. This can be in the form of an event, a person saying or doing something, or a new piece of information that is presented to us about something that we are seeking. Then, we are to wait until we reach clarity. Key your processing through listening, watching and waiting. Observe, receive, discuss and continue until you understand exactly what the Father is giving and how to interpret His will.

Psalm 143:8-12: Keep asking to be led and taught how to walk in His will.

8 Cause me to hear Your loving kindness in the morning, For in You do I trust; Cause me to know the way in which I should walk, For I lift up my soul to You. 9 Deliver me, O Lord, from my enemies; In You I take shelter. 10 Teach me to do Your will, For You are my God; Your Spirit is good. Lead me in the land of uprightness. 11 Revive me, O Lord, for Your

*name's sake! For Your righteousness' sake bring my soul out of trouble. 12
In Your mercy cut off my enemies, And destroy all those who afflict my soul;
For I am Your servant.*

As we seek His will, we continue to be encouraged to pray and ask
for His will. Ask to hear His voice, to be shown the way, to be delivered
from the roadblocks of the enemy, and to be taught His will which is
to lead us into the Promised Land. As we pray, we can expect to hear
Him. Keep praying, praying, praying.

Example: Peter & Cornelius: Acts 10

*1 There was a certain man in Caesarea called Cornelius, a centurion of
what was called the Italian Regiment, 2 a devout man and one who feared
God with all his household, who gave alms generously to the people, and
prayed to God always. 3 About the ninth hour of the day he saw clearly
in a vision an angel of God coming in and saying to him, "Cornelius!" 4
And when he observed him, he was afraid, and said, "What is it, lord?" So
he said to him, "Your prayers and your alms have come up for a memorial
before God. 5 Now send men to Joppa, and send for Simon whose surname
is Peter. 6 He is lodging with Simon, a tanner, whose house is by the sea. He
will tell you what you must do." 7 And when the angel who spoke to him
had departed, Cornelius called two of his household servants and a devout
soldier from among those who waited on him continually. 8 So when he
had explained all these things to them, he sent them to Joppa. 9 The next
day, as they went on their journey and drew near the city, Peter went up on
the housetop to pray, about the sixth hour. 10 Then he became very hungry
and wanted to eat; but while they made ready, he fell into a trance 11 and
saw heaven opened and an object like a great sheet bound at the four corners, descending to him and let down to the earth. 12 In it were all kinds
of four-footed animals of the earth, wild beasts, creeping things, and birds
of the air. 13 And a voice came to him, "Rise, Peter; kill and eat." 14 But
Peter said, "Not so, Lord! For I have never eaten anything common or unclean." 15 And a voice spoke to him again the second time, "What God has
cleansed you must not call common." 16 This was done three times. And
the object was taken up into heaven again. 17 Now while Peter wondered*

within himself what this vision which he had seen meant, behold, the men who had been sent from Cornelius had made inquiry for Simon's house, and stood before the gate. 18 And they called and asked whether Simon, whose surname was Peter, was lodging there. 19 While Peter thought about the vision, the Spirit said to him, "Behold, three men are seeking you. 20 Arise therefore, go down and go with them, doubting nothing; for I have sent them." 21 Then Peter went down to the men who had been sent to him from Cornelius, and said, "Yes, I am he whom you seek. For what reason have you come?" 22 And they said, "Cornelius the centurion, a just man, one who fears God and has a good reputation among all the nation of the Jews, was divinely instructed by a holy angel to summon you to his house, and to hear words from you." 23 Then he invited them in and lodged them. On the next day Peter went away with them, and some brethren from Joppa accompanied him. 24 And the following day they entered Caesarea. Now Cornelius was waiting for them, and had called together his relatives and close friends. 25 As Peter was coming in, Cornelius met him and fell down at his feet and worshiped him. 26 But Peter lifted him up, saying, "Stand up; I myself am also a man." 27 And as he talked with him, he went in and found many who had come together. 28 Then he said to them, "You know how unlawful it is for a Jewish man to keep company with or go to one of another nation. But God has shown me that I should not call any man common or unclean. 29 Therefore I came without objection as soon as I was sent for. I ask, then, for what reason have you sent for me?" 30 So Cornelius said, "Four days ago I was fasting until this hour; and at the ninth hourc I prayed in my house, and behold, a man stood before me in bright clothing, 31 and said, 'Cornelius, your prayer has been heard, and your alms are remembered in the sight of God. 32 Send therefore to Joppa and call Simon here, whose surname is Peter. He is lodging in the house of Simon, a tanner, by the sea. When he comes, he will speak to you.' 33 So I sent to you immediately, and you have done well to come. Now therefore, we are all present before God, to hear all the things commanded you by God." 34 Then Peter opened his mouth and said: "In truth I perceive that God shows no partiality. 35 But in every nation whoever fears Him and works righteousness is accepted by Him. 36 The word which God sent to the children of Israel, preaching peace through Jesus Christ—He is Lord of all— 37 that word you know, which was proclaimed throughout all Judea, and began from Galilee after the baptism which John preached: 38 how God anointed Jesus of Nazareth with the Holy Spirit and with power, who went about doing good and healing all who were oppressed by the devil, for God was with Him. 39 And we are witnesses of all things which He did both in the land of the Jews and in Jerusalem, whom theye killed by hanging on a tree. 40 Him God raised up on the third day, and showed Him openly, 41 not to all the people, but to witnesses chosen before by God, even to us who ate and drank with Him after He arose from the dead. 42 And He commanded us to preach to the people, and to testify that it is He who was ordained by God to be Judge of the living and the dead. 43 To Him all the prophets witness that, through His name, whoever believes in Him will receive remission of sins." 44 While Peter was still speaking these words, the Holy Spirit fell upon all those who heard the word. 45 And those of the circumcision who believed were astonished, as many as came with Peter, because the gift of the Holy Spirit had been poured out on the Gentiles also. 46 For they heard them speak with tongues and magnify God. Then Peter answered, 47 "Can anyone forbid water, that these should not be baptized who have received the Holy Spirit just as we have?" 48 And he commanded them to be baptized in the name of the Lord. Then they asked him to stay a few days.

This entire example is a beautiful description of how continuing to ask and seek leads us to God's will. Cornelius was wondering the about who God really was. He was given an instruction to go find Peter. At the same time, Peter was given a vision that was completely contrary to his paradigm–he could not fathom eating unclean food, so he could not accept God's first instruction to now eat of such. To his credit, he continued to ponder what this all meant since he did know the vision was from God.

The Holy Spirit instructed him to go with the men sent from Cornelius. Since Peter was used to hearing such instructions, he willingly went. As he heard continued to ponder what this all meant, he heard Cornelius' story. It all came together for him–the vision was not just about food, but about the gospel being opened to Gentiles–all the people of earth as God's nature is not to be partial. Cornelius, his family and his friends all now understood the true God and became believers in the Lord Jesus Christ, full of the Holy Spirit. God worked both sides of the deal, and both Cornelius and Peter joined His bigger story by continuing to seek His will (especially when not clear), being faithful to the steps revealed by God and experiencing the wonder of His will.

Confirm With The Father's Indicators:
Romans 14:17: Righteousness, peace and joy.

17 for the kingdom of God is not eating and drinking, but righteousness and peace and joy in the Holy Spirit.

As we continue to process and reach clarity about His will, He has given us built-in indicators of confirmation–righteousness, peace and joy. As we walk in Christ, in His righteousness, we will experience peace and joy. These are clear spiritual indicators that tell us we are on the right track. If we lack peace and joy, it just means that our hearts are troubled and we are to pay attention and seek further new information and new wisdom–realizing we aren't there yet.

2 Corinthians 3:17: Freedom.

17 Now the Lord is the Spirit; and where the Spirit of the Lord is, there is liberty.

Another key indicator is freedom. If we are burdened or troubled then we lack the freedom provided by the Holy Spirit. If we have clarity regarding His will, we will sense a free-ness and a confidence that we fully understand His will. We need to recognize that it is not a bad thing since He uses it as a way to confirm His will. If we lack freedom, again, it just means we need to keep going because we aren't there yet.

Matthew 18:18-20: Unity

18 Assuredly, I say to you, whatever you bind on earth will be bound in heaven, and whatever you loose on earth will be loosed in heaven. 19 Again I say to you that if two of you agree on earth concerning anything that they ask, it will be done for them by My Father in heaven. 20 For where two or three are gathered together in My name, I am there in the midst of them."

In addition to righteousness, peace, joy and freedom, God provides us another wonderful indicator—unity. If two of us agree then we can clearly pray for God to fulfill His will. Agreement, again, is not just between me and my spouse or me and another person, but is between me, my spouse or another person and God. Unity happens at the soul level through the Spirit. It means that we have come to a firm agreement without any doubt. It is clear and we are unified in that clarity.

It is a beautiful, built-in checker so that if our spouse or other important person or people in our life don't agree then, once again, we just aren't there yet and need to keep going. Unity is not something to be forced, but rather to be received freely. Stay in process until we reach unity; and when we reach unity with the Spirit and have righteousness peace, joy and freedom, we know they're there and then with great confidence move forward into His will. The Scriptures reveal wonderful truths about unity.

Psalm 133: God commands blessing.

1 A Song of Ascents. Of David. Behold, how good and how pleasant it is For brethren to dwell together in unity! 2 It is like the precious oil upon the head, Running down on the beard, The beard of Aaron, Running down on the edge of his garments. 3 It is like the dew of Hermon, Descending upon the mountains of Zion; For there the Lord commanded the blessing— Life forevermore.

When we reach unity together in Christ (through abiding), we discover His will, walk with Him into this will, and there He COMMANDS BLESSING. This is a very strong statement. It does not say that God suggests blessing or perhaps will decide to give us a blessing—

He commands blessing, so we are assured it will happen. Remember, it is not a negotiation or compromise, but rather is seeking together, with another like minded partner or friend (who also is abiding), what God speaks and desires. True unity. There, He commands blessing. Why would we not then go to unity?

Philippians 2:1-6: Process disagreement well.

1 Therefore if there is any consolation in Christ, if any comfort of love, if any fellowship of the Spirit, if any affection and mercy, 2 fulfill my joy by being like-minded, having the same love, being of one accord, of one mind. 3 Let nothing be done through selfish ambition or conceit, but in lowliness of mind let each esteem others better than himself. 4 Let each of you look out not only for his own interests, but also for the interests of others. 5 Let this mind be in you which was also in Christ Jesus, 6 who, being in the form of God, did not consider it robbery to be equal with God.

We are called to work to be of one accord and in harmony– within our soul and with the Holy Spirit. Paul actually tells us that it is necessary to look out for our own interests as we willingly consider other's interests. We are not called to just give in to avoid conflict or compromise or to short circuit open and frank discussion.

We are to look out for the other's interests just as we also look out for our own. Thus, we need to openly stay true to our own views, our own feelings, our own thoughts while, with respect and honor, we consider the other's views, feelings and thoughts. Then, together seek the will of the Father until both reach agreement at the soul level (your Spirit agrees and buys in), not just in the intellect.

It is important, and actually a good thing, to state our disagreement when we are not in unity with each other and with what we believe the Spirit to be revealing to us. As we hold to our true understanding at the moment, it should cause us to pursue further ask, seek and knock and listen, watch and wait in order to let the Father reveal His will to us step-by-step.

When we are in a place of disagreement, a valuable activity is to agree on what would be the next step in asking, seeking and knocking. Assign who is going to do the seeking for the new information or the new data and then come back and share what they've learned. Stay with it until we reach unity–God's will–a beautiful thing, with either our partner or a close friend.

Acts 1:14; 2:1; 2:42-46; 4:16-24; 5:12: One accord, agreement–gateway to the supernatural.

1:14 These all continued with one accord in prayer and supplication, with the women and Mary the mother of Jesus, and with His brothers.

2:1 When the Day of Pentecost had fully come, they were all with one accord in one place.

2:42 And they continued steadfastly in the apostles' doctrine and fellowship, in the breaking of bread, and in prayers. 43 Then fear came upon every soul, and many wonders and signs were done through the apostles. 44 Now all who believed were together, and had all things in common, 45 and sold their possessions and goods, and divided them among all, as anyone had need. 46 So continuing daily with one accord in the temple, and breaking bread from house to house, they ate their food with gladness and simplicity of heart,

16 saying, "What shall we do to these men? For, indeed, that a notable miracle has been done through them is evident to all who dwell in Jerusalem, and we cannot deny it. 17 But so that it spreads no further among the people, let us severely threaten them, that from now on they speak to no man in this name." 18 And they called them and commanded them not to speak at all nor teach in the name of Jesus. 19 But Peter and John answered and said to them, "Whether it is right in the sight of God to listen to you more than to God, you judge. 20 For we cannot but speak the things which we have seen and heard." 21 So when they had further threatened them, they let them go, finding no way of punishing them, because of the people, since they all glorified God for what had been done. 22 For the man was over forty years old on whom this miracle of healing had been performed. 23 And being let go, they went to their own companions and reported all that the chief priests and elders had said to them. 24 So when they heard that, they raised their voice to God with one accord and said: "Lord, You are God, who made heaven and earth and the sea, and all that is in them,

5: 12 And through the hands of the apostles many signs and wonders were done among the people. And they were all with one accord in Solomon's Porch.

The term, "One Accord" is a unique Greek word that helps us to understand the uniqueness of the Christian community. Ten of its 12 New Testament occurrences are in the Book of Acts. It is a compound of two words meaning to "rush along" and "in unison." The image is almost musical; a number of notes are sounded which, while different, harmonize in pitch and tone. Just as a concertmaster blends the varying instrumental sounds in a concert, the Holy Spirit blends together the lives of members of Christ's church.

In each situation described here, the church came together into one accord as they experienced God's supernatural work–His will for them; and drove us into the bigger story of bearing witness to God's glory and attracting people to the work of God, and thus to God Himself.

Proverbs 11:14; 19:20; 24:6: Godly counselors who will go to unity with us.

11:14 Where there is no counsel, the people fall; But in the multitude of counselors there is safety.

19:20 Listen to counsel and receive instruction, That you may be wise in your latter days.

24:6 For by wise counsel you will wage your own war, And in a multitude of counselors there is safety.

The Scriptures tell us that it is good to bring godly counselors around us who can help us get to unity. Usually, this godly counselor is our spouse or close friend. We are seeking unity with them, and thus confirming God's will. When we seem to experience an impasse or are in a place where God's will is not clear between two of us, then it is healthy to bring in a third party counselor. We do not want this counselor to give us their opinion or their best human advice–rather, we desire someone who will walk with us in seeking God's will and working through the process of asking, seeking and knocking until he or she can confirm in the Spirit what we see.

A good counselor asks good questions and opens up possibilities that perhaps we hadn't considered. He or she can also communicate wisdom regarding how to further seek God's will. A good counselor is invaluable and is why He set up the body. We are not to control each other, but rather to assist each other in seeking God's will. Never be afraid to invite a godly counselor into the process. As we seek God's will, we are looking for confirmation of God's will, and thus we are not looking for someone to confirm our position, but rather to help us reach God's will.

Malachi 3:16-18: Openly process, process, process.

16 Then those who feared the Lord spoke to one another, And the Lord listened and heard them; So a book of remembrance was written before Him For those who fear the Lord And who meditate on His name. 17 "They shall be Mine," says the Lord of hosts, "On the day that I make them My jewels. And I will spare them As a man spares his own son who serves him." 18 Then you shall again discern Between the righteous and the wicked, Between one who serves God And one who does not serve Him.

The truths here lift up the beauty of true prayer. It states that, while we are processing and discussing things together with those with whom we wish to seek unity, we are actually praying–God is hearing us. He answers our prayers through our processing. The more that we discuss and openly process the more insight, wisdom, revelation and secrets we will receive. It is a most beautiful thing to experience–open discussion is prayer.

This requires time and respectful hearts. We should have a desire to hear the other party's thoughts, opinions, beliefs and insights, as well as sharing our own. The more that we process back and forth the more clear things become–especially as the high moments come about what next step to take or what insight to pursue. Process, process, process. It is truly prayer, and God will answer our prayers.

2 Samuel 7:18-29: Stay with it until clear and known.

18 Then King David went in and sat before the Lord; and he said: "Who am I, O Lord God? And what is my house, that You have brought me this far? 19 And yet this was a small thing in Your sight, O Lord God; and You have also spoken of Your servant's house for a great while to come. Is this the manner of man, O Lord God? 20 Now what more can David say to You? For You, Lord God, know Your servant. 21 For Your word's sake, and according to Your own heart, You have done all these great things, to make Your servant know them. 22 Therefore You are great, O Lord God. For there is none like You, nor is there any God besides You, according to all that we have heard with our ears. 23 And who is like Your people, like Israel, the one nation on the earth whom God went to redeem for Himself as a people, to make for Himself a name—and to do for Yourself great and awesome deeds for Your land—before Your people whom You redeemed for Yourself from Egypt, the nations, and their gods? 24 For You have made Your people Israel Your very own people forever; and You, Lord, have become their God. 25 Now, O Lord God, the word which You have spoken concerning Your servant and concerning his house, establish it forever and do as You have said. 26 So let Your name be magnified forever, saying, 'The Lord of hosts is the God over Israel.' And let the house of Your servant David be established before You. 27 For You, O Lord of hosts, God of Israel, have revealed this to Your servant, saying, 'I will build you a house.' Therefore Your servant has found it in his heart to pray this prayer to You. 28 And now, O Lord God, You are God, and Your words are true, and You have promised this goodness to Your servant. 29 Now therefore, let it please You to bless the house of Your servant, that it may continue forever before You; for You, O Lord God, have spoken it, and with Your blessing let the house of Your servant be blessed forever."

The context here is that David had decided that it would be good idea for him to build God a permanent temple in Jerusalem versus moving the tabernacle from place to place. He went to Nathan the prophet to confirm, and Nathan agreed that it was a good idea. Then God took Nathan aside and said that they had not come and asked Him–and that David was not going to be allowed to build His temple.

However, God said, "I have a promise for David." God would build him a temple, and through his offspring would come the Kings of Israel and ultimately the Messiah, the Christ. As David was trying to understand the true meaning of this message, and thus God's will for him, he went through a deep processing. He found it in his heart to pray this promise (seeking insight and understanding) and stay with it until he understood and received three important ingredients of our prayers to possess the promises:

1. The giver of the promise was God Almighty–fully capable of fulfilling His promise because of His nature and His power.

2. The Word (the promise) was true–that everything that God speaks is true and that His word and promises are absolutely true. There is neither variation nor variability to His promises.

3. This promise has been given to and applied to specifically David. It is his alone.

So he stayed in this prayer until he fully understood the clarity of God's will (the promise), that God Himself was fully able to fulfill it, because He is God Almighty; and that this promise was specifically intended for him to possess. Based upon this process in reaching this point in his prayer life, he then could easily and confidently ask God to fulfill what He had spoken—in other words, to bring to reality what He had spoken in the Spirit. This is a wonderful process of prayer that must be adopted and followed in our prayers as we receive promises. We must follow the same three points until we reach the settling of these in our hearts so that we can then ask God to fulfill what He has spoken.

Example: David in Keilah 1 Samuel 23:1-13

1 Then they told David, saying, "Look, the Philistines are fighting against Keilah, and they are robbing the threshing floors." 2 Therefore David inquired of the Lord, saying, "Shall I go and attack these Philistines?" And the Lord said to David, "Go and attack the Philistines, and save Keilah." 3 But David's men said to him, "Look, we are afraid here in Judah. How much more then if we go to Keilah against the armies of the Philistines?" 4 Then David inquired of the Lord once again. And the Lord answered him and said, "Arise, go down to Keilah. For I will deliver the Philistines into your hand. 5 And David and his men went to Keilah and fought with the Philistines, struck them with a mighty blow, and took away their livestock. So David saved the inhabitants of Keilah. 6 Now it happened, when Abiathar the son of Ahimelech fled to David at Keilah, that he went down with an ephod in his hand. 7 And Saul was told that David had gone to Keilah. So Saul said, "God has delivered him into my hand, for he has shut himself in by entering a town that has gates and bars." 8 Then Saul called all the people together for war, to go down to Keilah to besiege David and his men. 9 When David knew that Saul plotted evil against him, he said to Abiathar the priest, "Bring the ephod here." 10 Then David said, "O Lord God of Israel, Your servant has certainly heard that Saul seeks to come to Keilah to destroy the city for my sake. 11 Will the men of Keilah deliver me into his hand? Will Saul come down, as Your servant has heard? O Lord God of Israel, I pray, tell Your servant." And the Lord said, "He will come down." 12 Then David said, "Will the men of Keilah deliver me and my men into the hand of Saul?" And the Lord said, "They will deliver you." 13 So David and his men, about six hundred, arose and departed from Keilah and went wherever they could go. Then it was told Saul that David had escaped from Keilah; so he halted the expedition.

David had already received a promise that He would be king. It was not quite working out that way. He was being chased by Saul and Saul's army with a goal of killing him. He wound up in a cave by himself and cried out to God, "How come this promise is not being fulfilled?" (We can read his lament in Psalm 142.) God sent his family to comfort him and then sent the society rejects for David to train as mighty warriors—his test of being faithful to small things. He was able to build a small army of 600 men—who were still being chased by Saul, and thus still hiding out in caves (in Israel, the caves were a bleak place to live—dry, hot, no shade, full of bugs—really unpleasant).

While hanging out in these caves, David learned that an Israel town was being attacked by the Philistines. David desired to know God's will and asked if he should protect the town. God said "yes." When David told his men, they said, "No way. We're not strong enough," and that Saul would find them and kill them. David could have said, "Sure. Makes sense. Let's not go," or, "God said to go, so we are going." He did neither. Rather, he knew that God did not mind confirming His will and would tell them all the answer. So he took his men and together asked God to reveal His will. (This is a great example of how it works with leadership, and especially with spouses—it is ok to disagree, but we should all go together with hearts to hear God's answers.) God reiterated to go and rescue Keilah and added another new revelation—God would deliver the enemy unto their hands. So they went, and God fulfilled His promise. They now were able to live again in a real town, have beds, food, recreation and fellowship—normal lives.

Then Saul discovered they were staying in Keilah and, being a town surrounded by mountains with only one way in or out through a gate, he could easily capture David and his men. This next step in seeking God's will is very important. David could have assumed that since God had rescued the town from the Philistines, He certainly would rescue David; or that since David and his men had rescued Keilah, the men of that town would prevent Saul from attacking David. This is called presumption—either based upon how God has acted in the past for us or based upon our own logic of what is expected to happen next.

However, David did not presume but, again, asked God to reveal His will. He asked if Saul was coming (if not then they could stay in the town, which was his and his men's preference). God said yes. Then, he asked if the men of Keilah would hand him over (though they should have protected him). God said, "Yes, time to go." This time, God was rescuing him by having him depart and avoid Saul's attack. David did not question this new instruction of God's will and departed—and was not attacked.

An interesting question is: Since the men never had a chance to hand David over, how did God know? God can play out all the consequences of our choices in a type of "virtual reality"—He can see it all and knows the outcomes of actions we take. David trusted God's answer and received His will without doubting. He knew that God was always willing to confirm His will (speak it to all involved who have hearts to hear) and not to presume any step. God knows and we don't. Seek His way every time, all the time!

The executive described in chapter 10 had put everything in order and was marching toward his retirement in the end of December—and he was quite excited about the adventure ahead. Then, in the fall, he received a phone call from the chairman to come to an important meeting. The chairman informed him that his counterpart in a second unit (company) had just been told that he had a serious medical issue and had to quit work immediately.

This was going to leave him the two main companies with limited experience in executive management and was asked to take over the President/CEO role of the second company, as the chairman understood that he wanted to reduce his travel and spend more time at home. The second company operation should afford him that opportunity. This was quite a curveball to the executive, who had already believed his retirement was confirmed by God. He had all things planned out for the next phase, which was agreed to by his wife and daughter. However, he understood that he was not to presume anything, but rather to continue to seek the Father's will, particularly when there was new information.

He walked through the process again. First he had to process what he knew to be true; he understood that he was still called to enter a new phase of life, to limit travel, spend more time at home and be available for his daughter in her final years of high school, including a trip to Oxford for a prolonged time of study and reflection. He knew that unless the job requirements could be adapted to him and his definition of working conditions, that it would not be God's will, since God had already spoken these things to him and his family. The father spoke that he, his wife and daughter should list all the conditions under which he would be willing to take on this new assignment. Their list of specific requirements was very lengthy and included simplified and reduced travel, and the important things to his wife and family that he had confirmed with God about how to live out his retirement.

He knew that the answer would be given by his knocking on the door and that the chairman would have to approve all of these, and if not then it was not God's will. He and his wife confirmed that if the chairman approved all these requirements, they both would feel confirmed in their spirit that it was God's will and that it would be in line with what they already knew to be true. Further, that if the chairman said no to even one of the requests that they would be thrilled that it was God's will to continue with their retirement plans. Having come to neutrality, it is such a beautiful experience to know that we can let God lead and not have to figure it out or compromise.

So, with the list in hand, he went to the chairman and the chairman said "yes" to all of it and only had one request—that the executive would commit to five years. He and his wife discussed this and agreed the most they could commit to was three, as their daughter was going to college in three years, so he said "no." The chairman agreed to the three years and confirmed he would honor his commitments (and he has). This is such a beautiful example of how to continue to walk with God, receiving his will step-by-step, and never presuming anything, including when the step takes a turn seemingly opposite of what we have thought. We have to remember that God's will is best and none better and that he doesn't tell us the entire will at once. Often this includes something that all of a sudden takes a major reversal or turn–God's way to get us to the next place. It is always going to be interesting and certainly exciting.

ONCE STEP IS CONFIRMED, THEN OBEDIENCE

Since God's will is progressive and revealed step-by-step, it is important for us to be obedient to the steps given. Each step is dependent on the previous step. If we ignore, neglect or refuse then we will be stalled out. God has a specific path where He directs our steps. Our role is to be obedient to those instructions and take the steps as they are given.

John 14:15-24: Obey = love, invites residence of God fully in me.

15 If you love Me, keep My commandments. 16 And I will pray to the Father, and He will give you another Helper, that He may abide with you forever— 17 the Spirit of truth, whom the world cannot receive, because it neither sees Him nor knows Him; but you know Him, for He dwells with you and will be in you. 18 I will not leave you orphans; I will come to you. 19 A little while longer and the world will see Me no more, but you will see Me. Because I live, you will live also. 20 At that day you will know that I am in My Father, and you in Me, and I in you. 21 He who has My commandments and keeps them, it is he who loves Me. And he who loves Me will be loved by My Father, and I will love him and manifest Myself to him.

Our obedience demonstrates our love for Him. He is the King and we are His subjects. Our role is to seek His will. We will further receive the next step of His will through obedience to each step. He confirms that the Holy Spirit will continue to guide us into truth and that we will experience the fullness of God within us, who will manifest Himself to us.

His will is to reveal His nature and His character in our everyday life through manifesting Himself in us, to us and through us—it requires our obedience. The words "keep His commandments" means that we carefully attend to and carefully follow exactly what He speaks to us. He asks us to pay attention and to carefully understand and obey each step. We must fully appreciate that obedience to the step leads us to the next step into His wonderful will. This is why we can demonstrate our love—we believe His will is best and none better and our step of obedience confirms that love.

John 15:9-15: Obey = joy to the full (His will).

9 "As the Father loved Me, I also have loved you; abide in My love. 10 If you keep My commandments, you will abide in My love, just as I have kept My Father's commandments and abide in His love. 11 These things I have spoken to you, that My joy may remain in you, and that your joy may be full. 12 This is My commandment, that you love one another as I have loved you. 13 Greater love has no one than this, than to lay down one's life for his friends. 14 You are My friends if you do whatever I command you. 15 No longer do I call you servants, for a servant does not know what his master is doing; but I have called you friends, for all things that I heard from My Father I have made known to you.

Obedience strengthens our abiding. As Christ obeyed the Father, He was brought closer into abiding in the Father. This means we will continue to hear His voice, receive His instruction and enjoy His fellowship. As our obedience keeps us in this place, Christ tells us that His joy is fulfilled—why? Because, we will have clarity regarding His instructions and will thus carry out His will, which is His grand purpose for us. We must fully appreciate that God loves to do His will. It is spectacular. It is best and none better. It demonstrates His glory and His power for us.

Deuteronomy 28:1-2; 15: Hear and obey = blessing; to not = cursing.

28:1 "Now it shall come to pass, if you diligently obey the voice of the Lord your God, to observe carefully all His commandments which I command you today, that the Lord your God will set you high above all nations of the earth. 2 And all these blessings shall come upon you and overtake you, because you obey the voice of the Lord your God:

28:15 "But it shall come to pass, if you do not obey the voice of the Lord your God, to observe carefully all His commandments and His statutes which I command you today, that all these curses will come upon you and overtake you:

Deuteronomy 28 sets forth the details of God's covenant—He will bless us to make us a blessing. It clearly states that if (Scripture always declares a condition) we hear His voice and are obedient to His instructions, all the blessings will come upon us. Our focus is not to be the blessing, but rather hearing His voice and being obedient to His voice. He further states (in verse 15) that if we are not willing to hear His voice and do not obey then curses will come upon us—not as punishment, but rather as consequences to our being disobedient. His invitation is always for us to repent and to choose to hear His voice and be obedient with the promise that the blessed abundant life will be given to us. Obedience is the key, and disobedience leads to living a life of trouble and leanness:

Psalm 106:13-15
They soon forgot His works; They did not wait for His counsel, 14 But lusted exceedingly in the wilderness, And tested God in the desert. 15 And He gave them their request, But sent leanness into their soul.

When we do not wait for His counsel (His purpose, His plans, His will) but seek (lust) our own way, we wind up testing God by asking Him to prove His love for us by giving us what we want. We receive the

160

leanness of our soul, and don't experience the abundance of His precious will. We need to fully understand that not caring and not waiting is disobedience and there are consequences.

Joshua 24:14-15; 24: Choice of the heart.

24:14 "Now therefore, fear the Lord, serve Him in sincerity and in truth, and put away the gods which your fathers served on the other side of the River and in Egypt. Serve the Lord! 15 And if it seems evil to you to serve the Lord, choose for yourselves this day whom you will serve, whether the gods which your fathers served that were on the other side of the River, or the gods of the Amorites, in whose land you dwell. But as for me and my house, we will serve the Lord."

24 And the people said to Joshua, "The Lord our God we will serve, and His voice we will obey!"

This obedience is a choice of the heart. It demonstrates whom we are serving. If we deny self and seek His will then we choose.

Examples: Joshua 1:1-9; 16-18; 5:13–15; 6:1-21; 7:1-26; 8:1-2; 30-35

1:1 After the death of Moses the servant of the Lord, it came to pass that the Lord spoke to Joshua the son of Nun, Moses' assistant, saying: 2 "Moses My servant is dead. Now therefore, arise, go over this Jordan, you and all this people, to the land which I am giving to them—the children of Israel. 3 Every place that the sole of your foot will tread upon I have given you, as I said to Moses. 4 From the wilderness and this Lebanon as far as the great river, the River Euphrates, all the land of the Hittites, and to the Great Sea toward the going down of the sun, shall be your territory. 5 No man shall be able to stand before you all the days of your life; as I was with Moses, so I will be with you. I will not leave you nor forsake you. 6 Be strong and of good courage, for to this people you shall divide as an inheritance the land which I swore to their fathers to give them. 7 Only be strong and very courageous, that you may observe to do according to all the law which Moses My servant commanded you; do not turn from it to the right hand or to the left, that you may prosper wherever you go. 8 This Book of the Law shall not depart from your mouth, but you shall meditate in it day and night, that you may observe to do according to all that is written in it. For then you will make your way prosperous, and then you will have good success. 9 Have I not commanded you? Be strong and of good courage; do not be afraid, nor be dismayed, for the Lord your God is with you wherever you go."

1:16 So they answered Joshua, saying, "All that you command us we will do, and wherever you send us we will go. 17 Just as we heeded Moses in all things, so we will heed you. Only the Lord your God be with you, as He was with Moses. 18 Whoever rebels against your command and does not heed your words, in all that you command him, shall be put to death. Only be strong and of good courage."

5:13 And it came to pass, when Joshua was by Jericho, that he lifted his eyes and looked, and behold, a Man stood opposite him with His sword drawn in His hand. And Joshua went to Him and said to Him, "Are You for us or for our adversaries?" 14 So He said, "No, but as Commander of the army of the Lord I have now come." And Joshua fell on his face to the earth and worshiped, and said to Him, "What does my Lord say to His servant?" 15 Then the Commander of the Lord's army said to Joshua, "Take your sandal off your foot, for the place where you stand is holy." And Joshua did so.

6:1 Now Jericho was securely shut up because of the children of Israel; none went out, and none came in. 2 And the Lord said to Joshua: "See! I have given Jericho into your hand, its king, and the mighty men of valor. 3 You shall march around the city, all you men of war; you shall go all around the city once. This you shall do six days. 4 And seven priests shall bear seven trumpets of rams' horns before the ark. But the seventh day you shall march around the city seven times, and the priests shall blow the trumpets. 5 It shall come to pass, when they make a long blast with the ram's horn, and when you hear the sound of the trumpet, that all the people shall shout with a great shout; then the wall of the city will fall down flat.

And the people shall go up every man straight before him." 6 Then Joshua the son of Nun called the priests and said to them, "Take up the Ark of the Covenant, and let seven priests bear seven trumpets of rams' horns before the ark of the Lord." 7 And he said to the people, "Proceed, and march around the city, and let him who is armed advance before the ark of the Lord." 8 So it was, when Joshua had spoken to the people, that the seven priests bearing the seven trumpets of rams' horns before the Lord advanced and blew the trumpets, and the ark of the covenant of the Lord followed them. 9 The armed men went before the priests who blew the trumpets, and the rear guard came after the ark, while the priests continued blowing the trumpets. 10 Now Joshua had commanded the people, saying, "You shall not shout or make any noise with your voice, nor shall a word proceed out of your mouth, until the day I say to you, 'Shout!' Then you shall shout." 11 So he had the ark of the Lord circle the city, going around it once. Then they came into the camp and lodged in the camp. 12 And Joshua rose early in the morning, and the priests took up the ark of the Lord. 13 Then seven priests bearing seven trumpets of rams' horns before the ark of the Lord went on continually and blew with the trumpets. And the armed men went before them. But the rear guard came after the ark of the Lord, while the priests continued blowing the trumpets. 14 And the second day they marched around the city once and returned to the camp. So they did six days. 15 But it came to pass on the seventh day that they rose early, about the dawning of the day, and marched around the city seven times in the same manner. On that day only they marched around the city seven times. 16 And the seventh time it happened, when the priests blew the trumpets, that Joshua said to the people: "Shout, for the Lord has given you the city! 17 Now the city shall be doomed by the Lord to destruction, it and all who are in it. Only Rahab the harlot shall live, she and all who are with her in the house, because she hid the messengers that we sent. 18 And you, by all means abstain from the accursed things, lest you become accursed when you take of the accursed things, and make the camp of Israel a curse, and trouble it. 19 But all the silver and gold, and vessels of bronze and iron, are consecrated to the Lord; they shall come into the treasury of the Lord." 20 So the people shouted when the priests blew the trumpets. And it happened when the people heard the sound of the trumpet, and the people shouted with a great shout, that the wall fell down flat. Then the people went up into the city, every man straight before him, and they took the city. 21 And they utterly destroyed all that was in the city, both man and woman, young and old, ox and sheep and donkey, with the edge of the sword.

7:1 But the children of Israel committed a trespass regarding the accursed things, for Achan the son of Carmi, the son of Zabdi, the son of Zerah, of the tribe of Judah, took of the accursed things; so the anger of the Lord burned against the children of Israel. 2 Now Joshua sent men from Jericho to Ai, which is beside Beth Aven, on the east side of Bethel, and spoke to them, saying, "Go up and spy out the country." So the men went up and spied out Ai. 3 And they returned to Joshua and said to him, "Do not let all the people go up, but let about two or three thousand men go up and attack Ai. Do not weary all the people there, for the people of Ai are few." 4 So about three thousand men went up there from the people, but they fled before the men of Ai. 5 And the men of Ai struck down about thirty-six men, for they chased them from before the gate as far as Shebarim, and struck them down on the descent; therefore the hearts of the people melted and became like water. 6 Then Joshua tore his clothes, and fell to the earth on his face before the ark of the Lord until evening, he and the elders of Israel; and they put dust on their heads. 7 And Joshua said, "Alas, Lord God, why have You brought this people over the Jordan at all—to deliver us into the hand of the Amorites, to destroy us? Oh, that we had been content, and dwelt on the other side of the Jordan! 8 O Lord, what shall I say when Israel turns its back before its enemies? 9 For the Canaanites and all the inhabitants of the land will hear it, and surround us, and cut off our name from the earth. Then what will You do for Your great name?" 10 So the Lord said to Joshua: "Get up! Why do you lie thus on your face? 11 Israel has sinned, and they have also transgressed My covenant which I commanded them. For they have even taken some of the accursed things, and have both stolen and deceived; and they have also put it among their own stuff. 12 Therefore the children of Israel could not stand before their enemies, but turned their backs before their enemies, because they have become doomed to destruction. Neither will I be with you anymore, unless you destroy the accursed from among you. 13 Get up, sanctify the people, and say, 'Sanctify yourselves for tomorrow, because thus says the Lord God of Israel: "There is an accursed thing in your midst, O Israel; you cannot stand before your enemies until you take away the accursed thing from among you." 14 In the morning therefore you shall be brought according to your tribes. And it shall be that the tribe which the Lord takes shall come according to families; and the family which the Lord takes shall come by households; and the household which the Lord takes shall come man by man. 15 Then it shall be that he who is taken with the accursed thing shall be burned with fire, he and all that he has, because he has transgressed the covenant of the Lord, and because he has done a disgraceful thing in Israel.'

" 16 So Joshua rose early in the morning and brought Israel by their tribes, and the tribe of Judah was taken. 17 He brought the clan of Judah, and he took the family of the Zarhites; and he brought the family of the Zarhites man by man, and Zabdi was taken. 18 Then he brought his household man by man, and Achan the son of Carmi, the son of Zabdi, the son of Zerah, of the tribe of Judah, was taken. 19 Now Joshua said to Achan, "My son, I beg you, give glory to the Lord God of Israel, and make confession to Him, and tell me now what you have done; do not hide it from me." 20 And Achan answered Joshua and said, "Indeed I have sinned against the Lord God of Israel, and this is what I have done: 21 "When I saw among the spoils a beautiful Babylonian garment, two hundred shekels of silver, and a wedge of gold weighing fifty shekels, I coveted them and took them. And there they are, hidden in the earth in the midst of my tent, with the silver under it." 22 So Joshua sent messengers, and they ran to the tent; and there it was, hidden in his tent, with the silver under it. 23 And they took them from the midst of the tent, brought them to Joshua and to all the children of Israel, and laid them out before the Lord. 24 Then Joshua, and all Israel with him, took Achan the son of Zerah, the silver, the garment, the wedge of gold, his sons, his daughters, his oxen, his donkeys, his sheep, his tent, and all that he had, and they brought them to the Valley of Achor. 25 And Joshua said, "Why have you troubled us? The Lord will trouble you this day." So all Israel stoned him with stones; and they burned them with fire after they had stoned them with stones. 26 Then they raised over him *a great heap of stones, still there to this day. So the Lord turned from the fierceness of His anger. Therefore the name of that place has been called the Valley of Achor to this day.*

8:1 Now the Lord said to Joshua: "Do not be afraid, nor be dismayed; take all the people of war with you, and arise, go up to Ai. See, I have given into your hand the king of Ai, his people, his city, and his land. 2 And you shall do to Ai and its king as you did to Jericho and its king. Only its spoil and its cattle you shall take as booty for yourselves. Lay an ambush for the city behind it."

8:30 Then Joshua built on Mount Ebal an altar to the LORD, the God of Israel, 31 as Moses the servant of the LORD had commanded the Israelites. He built it according to what is written in the Book of the Law of Moses—an altar of uncut stones, on which no iron tool had been used. On it they offered to the LORD burnt offerings and sacrificed fellowship offerings. 32 There, in the presence of the Israelites, Joshua copied on stones the law of Moses, which he had written. 33 All Israel, aliens and citizens alike, with their elders, officials and judges, were standing on both sides of the ark of the covenant of the LORD, facing those who carried it—the priests, who were Levites. Half of the people stood in front of Mount Gerizim and half of them in front of Mount Ebal, as Moses the servant of the LORD had formerly commanded when he gave instructions to bless the people of Israel. 34 Afterward, Joshua read all the words of the law—the blessings and the curses—just as it is written in the Book of the Law. 35 There was not a word of all that Moses had commanded that Joshua did not read to the whole assembly of Israel, including the women and children, and the aliens who lived among them.

After Moses and the nation of Israel miraculously crossed the red sea, they were given a promise by God (His will) that He would grant them the Promised Land. God stated that there was a large, powerful enemy in the land, but He would defeat them city by city; and they would live in victory and peace. The entire nation refused to go–they were too fearful and did not believe God's promise. Hebrews 3:15-19 states that God was angry with that generation for 40 years, and they could not enter the promise land because of their unbelief (refusal to be persuaded that what God promised was true).

So they wandered around for the 40 years and never experienced the will of God–in fact, all (except Caleb and Joshua who did believe) died outside God's will (remember, His will is always potential but not guaranteed). After Moses died, God invited the offspring (those born in the wilderness) to follow Caleb and Joshua into the same promise—to occupy the Promised Land. Joshua and Caleb said yes, and the entire new generation of Israelites said yes–willingly.

After crossing the Jordan (the name means "on bended knee–surrendered") Joshua learned an important lesson in God's will. The commander of the Lord's army (Jesus himself–not an angel, since Joshua was instructed he was on holy ground) came before Joshua. Joshua asked if he was for his plan or for the enemies plan. Jesus' response was simply no–and Joshua understood he had just asked the wrong question. As we seek God's will, it is not if God is for our plan or not, but rather if we want to purely follow God's plan.

So Joshua asked what Jesus had to say to his servant. Joshua got the question right–what was God's plan–period. Joshua now understood he was to follow God's instructions without question, and the promise would be fulfilled. He next received instructions to march around the walls of Jericho seven times and give a shout. Having understood complete surrender, Joshua simply obeyed. He had no plan B–and this was significant for a seasoned war general who would find God's plan of victory rather implausible. He did not reason it out–just followed.

However, he had another important lesson to learn. The next town was Ai–a small place that was easily conquered. So he assumed he would gain victory (since God had promised) and sent a small contingent of men to battle. They were routed. Joshua immediately understood he had made a major mistake–he forgot to check in and get his marching orders from God; and so he repented. God accepted his repentance and gave him forgiveness and then said that, had he checked in, he would have heard that there was sin the camp–that a family had disobeyed his instruction not to personally take anything from Jericho; the sin had to be dealt with (the entire family was killed) and then they could move on according to God's step-by-step plan.

Joshua never again took any steps on his own, but always inquired as to God's will. As a result he experienced victory each step of the way (though did compromise a few times) and the nation received the promise–they received the Promised Land and lived in peace. We too are to come to a complete surrender and continue to only follow His plan, not ours. We will discover this is best and none better!!

Years ago I was learning about the power of healing. Because of all the charlatans–particularly those who get on TV and tie healing to money (to them), I was somewhat jaded toward supernatural healing and tended to dismiss it. My thinking was that we have doctors and if they can't do it, then I guess that's God's will. The Father invited me to pursue this through abiding and being open to a deeper secret that his supernatural power was available to us. So I began by reading Andrew Murray's Divine Healing and camping out in the Scriptures presented in the book. I did lots of journaling and questioning about the depth of this meeting and the reality of this possibility.

In the middle of this, I experienced a very unusual situation. I was on my way to a meeting and Linda had asked me to stop at the store in the mall. I was running a little bit late so I was in a hurry. As the teller was checking me out, she could not finish the transaction. I stood there very impatiently and started snapping my fingers and asked my lady to hurry this along. She said, "Mr. I'm so sorry, but I cannot see the keyboard because of a migraine headache I've had for over a week." The Father said to me to lay hands on her and heal her. I said, "What?" I thought that there was no way, as it seemed unlikely that she would be healed and certainly not by me who was still a little skeptical. He said He would like to heal her.

I basically dismissed the notion and walked out to the car. As I got in the car, the father spoke to me and said, "Are you going to go back in there and lay hands on her, as I want to heal her?" It was such a strong message that I, in obedience, went back into the mall. I had to locate her and then ask her if it was okay if I laid hands on her, as God wanted to heal her of her migraine. She said, "Mr. whatever will work is fine with me." So I put my hand on her head, and I prayed this prayer, "Father, you said you wanted to heal her, so go ahead!"

She was healed and her migraine was gone. She said, "Oh my. I can see clearly, and it's absolutely gone." I asked her if she was a Christian, and she said she was but had drifted and didn't even go to church anymore. I said that this healing was not just a single benefit, but God calling her back to Him and that she was to get back to church and start learning to walk with Him. That small step of obedience was the beginning of His grander will of healing and supernatural opening up to me and my life. Having experienced it firsthand, I was more open to experiencing it further and to have Him reveal how supernatural living is to be normal and that he desires to reveal Himself in this way all the time.

I believe that had I not been obedient, this opportunity might have passed and I may never have stepped into the fullness of His will. I also have seen that his steps of obedience are always rather simple and tend to be small. He is teaching us to follow and to trust His steps so that we can experience all that He desires to do and be in our life. It is a grand walk, and obedience is a critical part.

15
CONCLUSION

1. Personal and planned out specifically for us.

2. Fully knowable—we can hear His voice receive His will.

3. Clear and precise—very specific.

4. Is simple and beautiful.

5. Does involve "character" being transformed—so all can know His voice from the most immature to the very mature Christians.

His will is as much about our becoming as our doing. He will transform us into His nature as we abide with Him and receive the transforming work of the Spirit. We will receive and enjoy the very nature of Christ living in us. Our character will be transformed into the nature of Christ as we abide. We are not to decide to obtain these qualities on our own—the more we try, the more we will fail, and thus get more discouraged and actually become less so. We, our spouses and our families will be able to testify if these are becoming stronger in our life or not. There is no standard, arbitrary definition of these to judge each other by. We will simply be growing in this fruit of the Spirit month after month. The changes will be obvious and a key indicator that we are abiding. We should care as much about this as we care about what we are to do.

6. Is best and none better—He is for us, has fantastic plans for us and invites us to enjoy a blessed life.

As we set our minds and hearts on the Spirit and are led by the Spirit, we will experience His supernatural work. We will be co-heirs with Christ and experience all the wonder and awe of His miraculous will for us. Our role is to follow Him knowing that His leading is taking us step-by-step into His wonderful and perfect will, where He will demonstrate and manifest His supernatural work.

7. Not limited to opening and closing doors.

8. Does take time, and timing is everything.

Hebrews 10:33-39: After we do His will–promises fulfilled.

The promises of God are contingent upon us following the instructions of His steps to His will. We must fully realize that His will is not a single event or end point, but rather a lifetime of steps where His promises will be fulfilled as we walk those steps. After we do the will of God, He fulfills His promises. We thus get to the right place with the right people at the right time where God does His miraculous supernatural work, which is His will. Our role is to be obedient and take each step as instructed. His role is actually His will–what He wishes to do in our life, through our life, for a lifetime.

I would like to end with a story that captures this summary. A couple that leads Living Waters retreats with us came with us to our 2015 leader retreat in Bavaria, Germany. One of the questions that they brought before the Lord was whether to stay in their house or sell it and move closer to their kids in a rental. At the retreat they both said they were in unity with each other–that they were to not sell and stay put. We asked them if they were in unity with the Spirit and at neutrality? They honestly said no, that it was their fleshly desire. We challenged that and they received it, knowing that God's will is best and none better.

The next day, after our time in the Word, we visited a beautiful Ludwig castle for sightseeing. The husband joined us, but the wife just went out into the beautiful gardens and dialogued with the Father–she journaled, spent time in the Word and wrestled through to surrendering her will and going to neutrality. After five hours she felt a release, a peaceful sense of neutrality, and heard the Father say to her to sell the home–he had a grand place for her already picked out. She just shared with her husband that she was at neutrality, but nothing about what she heard. Knowing the Spirit is One, she asked her husband to go to neutrality and ask the Father to speak to him; and that if she heard correctly, he would hear the same thing–and she continued to pray to seek His will and not presume anything at that point. God would let them know and it would be grand!!

The next morning he had a dream, and it revealed that they should sell their home. He shared that with his wife and she confirmed what she heard, presented to the group, and we all, in the Spirit, confirmed that was God's will. A realtor's name came to mind and they called overseas; she was a believer who said she could give it priority. It just so happened that their maid was at the house and could let the realtor in to get it ready for showing, get a key and get it on the market. She did all that in two days and it was listed (both had received the price from the Lord) while they were in Germany. As this was being set up, they began to wonder if any good property was available for them to rent. We all encouraged them to spend time together defining what would be a grand place for them to rent, so that coming home everyday would be a true joy.

They left the retreat with the house listed, open for showings and processing through defining their heart's desire for the new rental–and on they went to a cruise in the Balkans. While cruising (where there was supposedly no cell signal), they received a call that the house sold for full price and they had to process the paperwork while on the cruise ship (which miraculously they were able to do). AND, the buyer had to close in three weeks, so when they returned they had to find a place and move–in three weeks!!

Returning home, they started looking and were a little discouraged. It seemed like rentals were not that great and perhaps they would have to settle for less than desired–but oh well, at least they sold their house. The realtor suggested they see this one very large house with a guest house on the grounds. The price was above their range, but the Christian realtor encouraged them to look and believe God. They did, and it truly was spectacular but higher than they could afford. The realtor prayed with them and they made an offer that was affordable to them. The landlord accepted it!! And within four weeks of being at our retreat in Germany–they heard God's will, were obedient to His will, sold their house and moved into the grand place that God had ordained for them. Whew!! How amazing is that? We all were privileged in experiencing God at work and how beautiful His life is for us as we went to neutrality and let Him guide us–is best and none better!

AUTHOR BIO

As a ministry leader, Richard T. Case received his seminary Masters Degree from Trinity Evangelical Divinity School, Summa Cum Laude.

He has served as interim pastor for several troubled churches, bringing reconciliation and new vision to these situations. He and his wife Linda have also planted several new churches which remain strong. Currently, he and Linda lead a fruitful, Christian marriage retreat ministry – "All for Jesus Living Waters Retreat Ministry." They now have trained over a dozen couples as leaders who are conducting marriage retreats in their respective geographies around the country.

Mr. Case has served as a strategic consultant to numerous non-profit organizations, including CEO FORUM, Focus on the Family, and Navigators.

As a business Executive, Mr. Case is a 42 year Fortune 500 veteran, having served with companies such as Baxter Laboratories, Corning Glass Works and American Hospital Supply. Richard has also provided consulting services to numerous industries in areas of capital raising, business turnaround, strategic planning, M&A, operational analysis, product development, strategic and international marketing and development, product development, organizational behavior, and culture change. Case is a featured speaker at numerous conferences and seminars and management training venues.

Mr. Case has received The Wall Street Journal Achievement Award, and is listed in Who's Who in American Business.

Richard lives in Castle Rock, Colorado with his wife of 43 years. They both enjoy their five grand children and their three grown children.

elevate
publishing

DELIVERING TRANSFORMATIVE MESSAGES
TO THE WORLD

Visit www.elevatepub.com for our latest offerings.

NO TREES WERE HARMED IN THE MAKING OF THIS BOOK.

OK, so a few did make the ultimate sacrifice.

In order to steward our environment, we are partnered with *Plant With Purpose*, to plant a tree for every tree that paid the price for the printing of this book.

To learn more, visit www.elevatepub.com/about

PLANT W TH PURPOSE | WWW.PLANTWITHPURPOSE.ORG

CPSIA information can be obtained
at www.ICGtesting.com
Printed in the USA
FSOW02n0513140218
44328FS